CAMBRIDGE
UNIVERSITY PRESS

CAMBRIDGE PRIMARY
Global Perspectives

Teacher's Resource 1

Adrian Ravenscroft & Achama Mathew

CAMBRIDGE
UNIVERSITY PRESS

Shaftesbury Road, Cambridge CB2 8BS, United Kingdom

One Liberty Plaza, 20th Floor, New York, NY 10006, USA

477 Williamstown Road, Port Melbourne, VIC 3207, Australia

314–321, 3rd Floor, Plot 3, Splendor Forum, Jasola District Centre, New Delhi – 110025, India

103 Penang Road, #05–06/07, Visioncrest Commercial, Singapore 238467

Cambridge University Press is part of the University of Cambridge.

It furthers the University's mission by disseminating knowledge in the pursuit of education, learning and research at the highest international levels of excellence.

www.cambridge.org
Information on this title: www.cambridge.org/9781109354165

First published 2024

20 19 18 17 16 15 14 13 12 11 10 9 8 7 6 5 4 3

Printed in the UK by CPI Group (UK) Ltd, Croydon CR04YY

A catalogue record for this publication is available from the British Library

ISBN 978-1-109-35416-5 Teacher's Resource 1 Paperback with Digital Access

Additional resources for this publication at www.cambridge.org/GO

Cover illustration: Omar Aranda (Beehive Illustration).

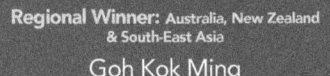

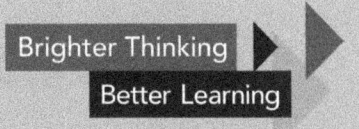

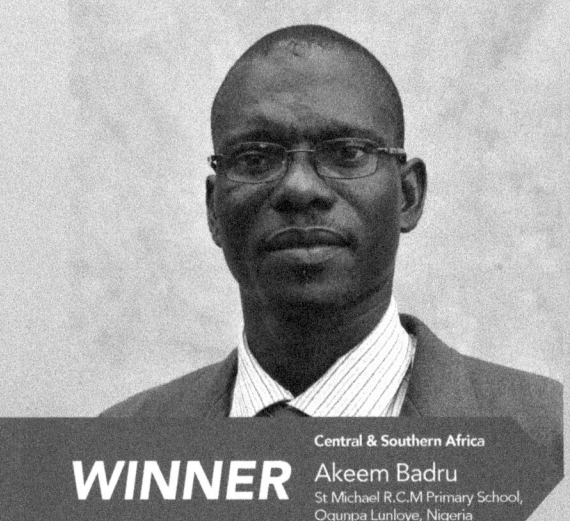

Endorsement statement

Endorsement indicates that a resource has passed Cambridge International's rigorous quality-assurance process and is suitable to support the delivery of a Cambridge International curriculum framework. However, endorsed resources are not the only suitable materials available to support teaching and learning, and are not essential to be used to achieve the qualification. Resource lists found on the Cambridge International website will include this resource and other endorsed resources.

Any example answers to questions taken from past question papers, practice questions, accompanying marks and mark schemes included in this resource have been written by the authors and are for guidance only. They do not replicate examination papers. In examinations the way marks are awarded may be different. Any references to assessment and/or assessment preparation are the publisher's interpretation of the curriculum framework requirements. Examiners will not use endorsed resources as a source of material for any assessment set by Cambridge International.

While the publishers have made every attempt to ensure that advice on the qualification and its assessment is accurate, the official curriculum framework, specimen assessment materials and any associated assessment guidance materials produced by the awarding body are the only authoritative source of information and should always be referred to for definitive guidance. Cambridge International recommends that teachers consider using a range of teaching and learning resources based on their own professional judgement of their students' needs.

Cambridge International has not paid for the production of this resource, nor does Cambridge International receive any royalties from its sale. For more information about the endorsement process, please visit www.cambridgeinternational.org/endorsed-resources

Third party websites and resources referred to in this publication have not been endorsed by Cambridge Assessment International Education.

Contents

Digital resources

The following items are available on Cambridge GO. For more information on how to access and use your digital resource, please see inside front cover.

- Active learning
- Assessment for learning
- Developing learners' language skills
- Differentiation
- Improving learning through questioning
- Language awareness
- Metacognition
- Skills for Life
- Downloadable resources, assessment guidance, worksheets and audio transcripts.

> Introduction

Welcome to the *Cambridge Primary Global Perspectives Teacher's Resource 1*, intended for use alongside *Cambridge Primary Global Perspectives Learner's Skills Book 1*.

Being a classroom teacher is not an easy job. Children are growing up in a complex, fast-changing and interconnected world. The best teachers understand that their job is to help the children make sense of it. Cambridge Primary Global Perspectives is an innovative programme. It is designed to help you teach young children a range of key skills.

These skills have been identified as being of core importance in successfully navigating and thriving in this challenging environment. The programme identifies six key Cambridge Global Perspectives™ skills. These are: Research, Analysis, Evaluation, Reflection, Collaboration and Communication.

The opening sections of this Teacher's Resource contain guidance about how to approach Cambridge Primary Global Perspectives. We will consider:

- how to incorporate Cambridge Primary Global Perspectives into the wider curriculum
- how to support learners for whom English is an additional language (EAL)
- how to support children with a wide range of prior attainment.

A real joy of teaching Cambridge Primary Global Perspectives to young children is that children of this age are at an early stage in the process of developing their sense of the world. They are used to doing this independently and by engaging with other children.

As educators, we want this to be a lifelong process. We take the view that the best way to develop and refine these core skills is by applying them practically.

Our materials are designed to help you structure a journey of discovery for the children you teach. The chapters of the Learner's Skills Book are dedicated to four practical projects. Each practical project has a defined outcome – for example, producing a model garden and discussing its features, or participating in a role play about a workplace and explaining what is being done. Working towards each outcome requires learners to complete activities that give them opportunities to practise and develop all of the core skills.

The later sections of this book mirror the structure of the Learner's Skills Book. For each project, there are sections containing teaching notes relating to each of the lessons in the Learner's Skills Book. Detailed guidance sets out each of the activities.

Detailed notes will help teachers to plan lessons that take account of the needs of groups of learners and individuals. Shared learning outcomes are set out in child-friendly language. Suggested 'support' and 'extra challenge' activities will help teachers to carefully match teaching and learning activities and resources to support children in achieving these intended learning outcomes.

There are also a range of downloadable resources available to support teaching and learning. These can be found online at http://cambridge.org/go

During the course of the four projects, the course materials will enable teachers and learners to experience a variety of approaches to teaching and learning.

We hope to support you as an effective facilitator of Cambridge Global Perspectives. We want you to show your learners where to look but not necessarily what to see. We hope you will enjoy helping them to explore new ideas in the classroom and in the community. Hopefully, you will find this process of helping learners to become empowered, reflective and engaged global citizens a rewarding one.

Cambridge Global Perspectives involves learners in learning about the world around them; the impact of global issues on their local area and different perspectives on how best to resolve these issues. You may need to involve learners in communicating with people in the wider community, conducting research off-site and exchanging ideas with learners in contrasting settings. All off-site visits must be risk assessed and carried out in accordance with relevant school health and safety policies. All communication must be conducted in line with school safeguarding and e-safety policies.

About the authors

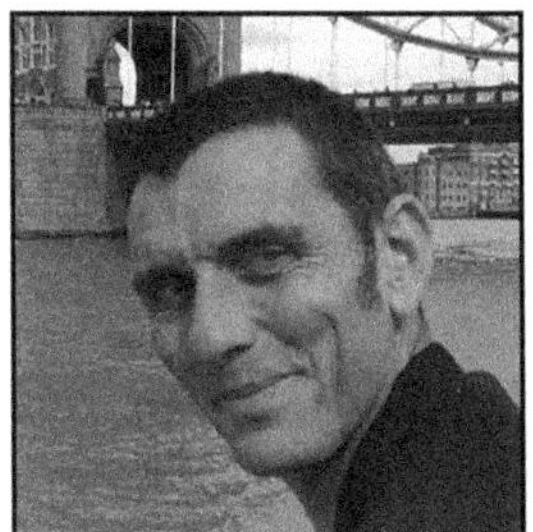

Adrian Ravenscroft

Adrian Ravenscroft has worked as a teacher, teacher trainer and as an education consultant and assessment specialist. After gaining his degree in Government from the University of Essex, he trained to be a teacher at Sheffield City Polytechnic. He began his teaching career in Bradford before returning to work in his native Birmingham. During his career, he has successfully taught children in Primary, Middle and Secondary schools. Following his research, (which focused on the comparative study of citizenship education), he was awarded a Master's degree in Education from the University of Leeds. He has provided bespoke tutorial support for Teaching Assistants which enabled them to successfully gain Qualified Teacher Status. He has also provided professional development for teachers in 15 countries. In addition to this Stage 1 guide, his other published work includes innovative resources in Cambridge Global Perspectives for teachers and students working at Upper Primary and IGCSE level. He has contributed to three episodes of Cambridge's 'Brighter Thinking' podcast and is a member of the Writers' Guild of Great Britain.

Achama Mathew

Achama Mathew graduated in Psychology and completed postgraduate study in Special Education. She has also done the CIDTL and is an experienced Cambridge Primary Global Perspectives teacher. She has been in the field of education for 38 years and works as the Chief Education Officer for the Bombay Cambridge Gurukul Schools. Achama works on the instructional design of the curriculum and is involved with strategic planning, ensuring that a positive learning environment is established for both learners and teachers. As a Special Educator, she has striven to facilitate mainstreaming of learners with special needs to give them the best opportunity in the school system. She is also a trainer for Primary and Lower Secondary Global Perspectives. As a trainer, she enjoys enhancing teachers' skills in order to facilitate greater classroom effectiveness.

How to use this series

This suite of resources supports learners and teachers following the Cambridge Primary Global Perspectives curriculum framework (0838) from 2022. The components in the series are designed to work together and help learners develop the necessary skills for this subject. With clear language and style, they are designed for international learners.

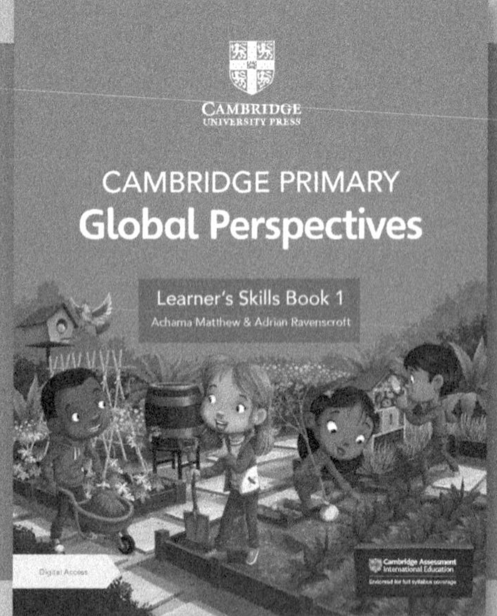

The Learner's Skills Book is designed for learners to use in class with guidance from the teacher. It offers complete coverage of Cambridge Primary Global Perspectives. The Learner's Skills Book supports learners in developing the Global Perspectives skills of analysis, collaboration, communication, evaluation, reflection and research through an active learning approach. Each project also provides opportunities to practise the Global Perspectives skills through audio-visual content, engaging topics, discussion activities and independent reflection.

A digital version of the Learner's Skills Book is included with the print version and is available separately.

The Teacher's Resource provides everything teachers need to confidently deliver the course. It is packed full of useful teaching notes and lesson plans, with suggestions for differentiation to support and challenge learners, and ideas for formative assessment.

A digital version of the Teacher's Resource is included with the print version. The digital resource contains worked examples and templates for activities which give learners further opportunities to develop the six Global Perspectives skills through interesting projects.

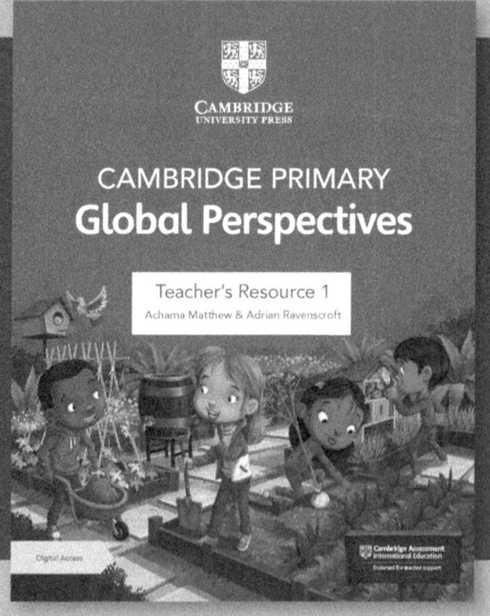

> How to use this Teacher's Resource

This Teacher's Resource contains both general guidance and teaching notes that will help you to deliver the content for Cambridge Primary Global Perspectives Stage 1.

There are teaching notes for each project in the Learner's Skills Book. A full set of teaching notes will help you deliver each of the six lessons in the project.

The notes for each project begin with an introduction, which describes the learning journey that the learners will undertake. This sets out how each of the skills will be drawn upon in the project. The introduction will also help you to structure the development of learners' metacognitive understanding by explaining the skills developed in each lesson. It also includes a list of skills that it is useful if the learners have as they begin the project.

At the start of each lesson is a summary of the relevant Cambridge **learning objectives** and learning goals for the lesson. The learning objectives box shows you which objectives from the curriculum framework the lesson addresses.

LEARNING OBJECTIVES: ANALYSIS

1A.01 Identifying perspectives: Say something known about an issue

The lesson **learning goals** feature shows you the learner-friendly goals as they are set out in the Learner's Skills Book.

LEARNING GOALS

- I can say who is in my family.

There is also a box showing which of the Cambridge **learner attributes** the lesson helps learners to develop.

LEARNING ATTRIBUTES

This lesson gives learners the opportunity to be:

- Confident in working with information and ideas – their own and those of others.

A list of **resources** required – including the relevant pages from the Learner's Skills Book, downloadable resources, and audio and video material – is provided for each lesson.

> **Resources needed**
>
> Learners to bring a photograph or a drawing of their family members
>
> Learner's Skills Book pages 8–13
>
> Downloadable 1.1 (photos of different kinds of families)

The teaching notes for each lesson include an idea for a **Starter** activity. This provides a way of activating learners' prior understanding. Suggestions are also given here about how you can conduct some initial formative assessment and identify any misunderstandings that might exist. They also allow you to work out which learners might need additional support to meet the goals – or further challenge.

> **Starter**
>
> **Good for:** Recapping the learning about family relationships from Getting Started to help learners with the activities in this lesson
>
> **Activity:** Ask learners if they can remember the photos of Arun, Sofia and Marcus's families. Conduct a quick quiz: say the name of the character (Arun, Sofia or Marcus) and learners have to name a member of their family who appeared in the picture.

The **activities** in the Learner's Skills Book are set out in turn with suggested ways of working.

> **What can we do in a garden?**
>
> **Good for:** Learners to gain confidence in talking about the issue of gardens; their similarities and differences.
>
> **Activity:** Ask learners to work with a partner. They should look at the three photos and discuss the four questions together. Take feedback as a class.

Suggested answers and/or **worked examples** are provided to help you model what is expected or give good feedback. This serves as an example of what success looks like. Remember though that this is a skills-based course and a variety of successful answers are frequently acceptable.

> **Answers and formative assessment:** Answers will depend on each learner's individual family and circumstances. Check whether learners are able to identify and share the name of a family member and explain how they are addressed.

In the **Differentiation** section, you will find advice on providing extra support or extra challenge in response to the attainment demonstrated by your learners'.

> **Differentiation:**
>
> Give support by helping learners with spelling (e.g. telling learners to look for spellings of family relationships from the pictures in Getting Started or writing out the common ones on the board for learners to copy). If learners have specific family names that they would like to include, suggest that they ask for help from their family at home.

The **Plenary** section contains guidance about how to help learners reflect on what has been learned.

> Plenary
>
> **Activity:** Display the following statements about the interview with the visitor (or adapt them to match what you did):

Where appropriate, suggestions are provided for how learners can further develop and reinforce their understanding through learning outside the classroom. Suggestions are provided for how you might communicate with parents to promote home learning.

> Home learning ideas
>
> **Activity:** Learners interview a family member (or other appropriate adult) at home. Ask learners to share orally who they will interview. Ask them to think about: What five questions will they ask? Whose help will they ask for at home to record the interview?

At the end of each project is a **Taking it further** section in which you will find suggestions for how you can enrich learning.

Where appropriate, links between the teaching and learning in these materials and suggested in the Taking it further section of each project.

> ## Taking it further
>
> This project will have helped learners to explore the different kinds of families that there are and the role that families play in their growing up years. The project also has the potential to build closer and fruitful ties between the school and the families of the learners.

Register to access free supporting resources, including assessment guidance, worked examples and activity templates, through Cambridge GO – the home for all your Cambridge digital content. Visit cambridge.org/go

About the curriculum framework

The information in this section is based on the Cambridge Primary Global Perspectives curriculum framework (0838) from 2022. You should always refer to the appropriate curriculum framework document for the year of your learners' assessment to confirm the details and for more information.
Visit the Cambridge Primary Support Site at www.cambridgeinternational.org/primary to find out more.

Cambridge Primary Global Perspectives is a skills-based programme. It brings together understanding from a range of subjects from across a broad and balanced primary curriculum. Crucially for young learners, the programme aims to help them to make sense of the world for themselves. A key approach is the fostering of independent learning. Young learners are encouraged to develop the necessary skills that will help them as they grow to consider and connect different perspectives on global issues.

The learning objectives for Cambridge Primary Global Perspectives are divided into six strands. Each strand corresponds to one of the six key skills that the course aims to develop:

- analysis
- collaboration
- communication
- evaluation
- reflection
- research.

Separate sets of learning objectives are provided for Stage 1, Stage 2, Stages 3–4 and Stages 5–6.

It is important to recognise that there is no prescribed content for Cambridge Primary Global Perspectives. Children do not have to learn facts. The focus is on developing the six skills. Learners should be given opportunities to develop and practise these skills. This will help them to explore their own developing perspectives on issues that have an impact in the community served by your school.

Learners should explore a range of issues. The curriculum framework suggests that learners might focus on some of the following topics:

- Digital world
- Education for all
- Family, friends, community and culture
- Globalisation
- Health and wellbeing
- Improving communication
- Looking after planet Earth
- Moving goods and people
- Moving to a new country
- Obeying the law
- Rich and poor
- Sport and recreation
- The world of work
- Values and beliefs
- Water, food and farming
- Working with other countries.

In addition to the Cambridge Primary Global Perspectives curriculum framework, Cambridge International provides a set of challenges. These resources provide suggestions for ways in which teachers can help their learners practise their Cambridge Primary Global Perspectives skills. Information about the Cambridge Challenges can be found on the Cambridge Primary Support Site.

> Curriculum mapping

The information in this section is based on the Cambridge Primary Global Perspectives curriculum framework (0838) from 2022. You should always refer to the appropriate curriculum framework document for the year of your learners' assessment to confirm the details and for more information. Visit the Cambridge Primary Support Site to find out more.

The mapping grids below show how the Learner's Skills Book and accompanying downloadable resources made available with this Teacher's Resource can be used to support your delivery of the Cambridge Primary Global Perspectives curriculum framework. They show how the learning goals for each lesson in the Learner's Skills Book map to and provide comprehensive coverage of the learning objectives listed in the curriculum framework.

They also show which of the Cambridge Primary Global Perspectives topics and challenges the projects are most closely related to and the skills that are the assessment focus for each project (see detailed guidance in the following table). The mapping grids also show the United Nations Sustainable Development Goals and the articles of the United Nations Convention on the Rights of the Child that could be explored in conjunction with each project.

1 What can families teach us?

Outcome	A display in which learners share what they have learned from older family members.
Challenge(s)	Growing and growing up; Learning new things.
Curriculum topic(s)	Family, friends, community and culture; Education for all.
UN Sustainable Development Goal	UN Sustainable Development Goal 4: Ensure inclusive and equitable quality education and promote lifelong learning opportunities for all.
UN Rights of the Child	• Article 5: You have the right to be given guidance by your parents and family. • Article 9: You have the right to live with your parents, unless it is bad for you. • Article 18: You have the right to be brought up by your parents, if possible.
Skills focus for assessment	Communication: 1Cm.01, 1Cm.02

Lesson	Learning goals	Learning objectives	Learner Attributes
1.1	Analysis and Research		
	• I can say who is in my family. • I can find out if we all use the same names for family members.	1A.01 Identifying perspectives: Say something known about an issue. 1A.02 Interpreting data: Talk about information recorded in pictograms or graphic organisers. 1Rs.01 Constructing research questions: Ask basic questions about a given issue.	Confident in working with information and ideas – their own and those of others.
1.2	Communication and Research		
	• I can talk about what I have learned from family members. • I can record answers in a chart.	1Cm.01 Communicating information: Answer questions with relevant information about a given issue. 1Rs.04 Recording findings: Record information on a given issue in pictograms or simple graphic organisers.	Responsible for themselves, responsive to and respectful of others.
1.3	Research and Evaluation		
	• I can ask questions to find out about people's lives	1Rs.01 Constructing research questions: Ask basic questions about a given issue. 1Rs.02 Information skills: Talk about information on a given issue in sources provided. 1Rs.03 Conducting research: Begin to participate in simple investigations and ask basic questions to find information and opinions. 1E.01 Evaluating sources: Select a source relevant to a given issue and explain reasons for choice.	Confident in working with information and ideas – their own and those of others.
1.4	Reflection		
	• I can learn stories, games and interesting facts from older people.	1Rf.03 Personal perspectives: Talk about what has been learned during an activity, with support.	Engaged intellectually and socially, ready to make a difference.
1.5	Communication and Analysis		
	• I can show other people what I have learned from my family.	1Cm.01 Communicating information: Answer questions with relevant information about a given issue. 1Cm.02 Listening and responding: Listen to others in class discussions and respond with simple questions. 1A.04 Solving problems: Choose a possible solution to an issue from a range of actions given.	Confident in working with information and ideas – their own and those of others.
1.6	Reflection		
	• I can talk about something I liked.	1Rf.03 Personal learning: Talk about what has been learned during an activity with support. 1Rf.04 Personal perspectives: Talk about something liked in a particular activity.	Reflective as learners, developing their ability to learn.

2 What kind of garden would be best?

Outcome	The learners make a model of a school garden and explain what it represents.
Challenge(s)	Fun with fruits; Looking after our world.
Curriculum topic(s)	Water, food and farming; Looking after planet Earth.
UN Sustainable Development Goals	• UN Sustainable Development Goal 15: Protect, restore and promote sustainable use of terrestrial ecosystems, sustainably manage forests, combat desertification, halt and reverse land degradation and halt biodiversity loss. • UN Sustainable Development Goal 2: End hunger, achieve food security and improved nutrition and promote sustainable agriculture.
UN Rights of the Child	• Article 12: Every child has the right to express their views, feelings and wishes in all matters affecting them, and to have their views considered and taken seriously. • Article 24: Every child has the right to the best possible health. Governments must provide good quality health care, clean water, nutritious food, a clean environment and education on health and wellbeing so that children can stay healthy. Richer countries must help poorer countries achieve this.
Skills focus for assessment	Evaluation: 1E.01, 1E.02 Research: 1Rs.03, 1Rs.04

Lesson	Learning goals	Learning objectives	Learner Attributes
2.1	Analysis		
	• I can say what I know about gardens.	**1A.01** Identifying perspectives: Say something known about an issue.	Confident in working with information and ideas – their own and those of others.
2.2	Research		
	• I can make a chart that shows children's ideas.	**1Rs.01** Constructing research questions: Ask basic questions about a given issue. **1Rs.03** Conducting research: Begin to participate in simple investigations and ask basic questions to find information and opinions. **1 Rs.04** Recording findings: Record information on a given issue in pictograms or simple graphic organisers.	Responsible for themselves, responsive to and respectful of others.
2.3	Evaluation		
	• I can choose a good source of facts and ideas about gardens.	**1E.01** Evaluating sources: Select a source relevant to a given issue and explain reasons for choice.	Reflective as learners, developing their ability to learn.

Lesson	Learning goals	Learning objectives	Learner Attributes
2.4	Collaboration and Analysis		
	• I can work with my group to make a model of a school garden.	1Cl.01 Working together: Work positively with others, sharing resources while working independently or with others. 1A.04 Solving problems: Choose a possible solution to an issue from a range of actions given. 1E.02 Evaluating perspectives and arguments: State an opinion about a given issue.	Innovative and equipped for new and future challenges.
2.5	Communication		
	• I can talk about our model gardens.	1Cm.01 Communicating information: Answer questions with relevant information about a given issue. 1Cm.02 Listening and responding: Listen to others in class discussions and respond with simple questions.	Engaged intellectually and socially, ready to make a difference.
2.6	Reflection		
	• I can talk about what I learned. • I can talk about something I liked.	1Rf.03 Personal perspectives: Talk about what has been learned during an activity with support. 1Rf.04 Personal learning: Talk about something liked in a particular activity.	Reflective as learners, developing their ability to learn.

3 What do we know about jobs?

Outcome	The learners present a role play about a place of work and answer questions.
Challenge(s)	Working and having a job; Working together.
Curriculum topic(s)	The world of work; Improving communication.
UN Sustainable Development Goal	• UN Sustainable Development Goal 8: Promote sustained, inclusive and sustainable economic growth, full and productive employment and decent work for all.
UN Rights of the Child	• Article 32: Governments must protect children from economic exploitation and work that is dangerous or might harm their health, development or education. Governments must set a minimum age for children to work and ensure that work conditions are safe and appropriate.
Skills focus for assessment	Research: 1Rs.01, 1Rs.02 Reflection: 1Rf.01, 1Rf.02, 1Rf.03, 1Rf.04 Collaboration: 1Cl.01

Lesson	Learning goals	Learning objectives	Learner Attributes
3.1	Analysis		
	• I can talk about different jobs that people do.	1A.01 Identifying perspectives: Say something known about an issue.	Confident in working with information and ideas – their own and those of others.
3.2	Research		
	• I can ask questions about jobs.	1Rs.01 Constructing research questions: Ask basic questions about a given issue. 1Rs.02 Information skills: Talk about information on a given issue in sources provided. 1Rs.03 Conducting research: Begin to participate in simple investigations and ask basic questions to find information and opinions.	Responsible for themselves, responsive to and respectful of others
3.3	Evaluation		
	• I can choose a good source of facts and ideas about jobs. • I can give my opinion about what I have found out.	1E.01 Evaluating sources: Select a source relevant to a given issue and explain reasons for choice. 1E.02 Evaluating perspectives and arguments: State an opinion about a given issue.	Reflective as learners, developing their ability to learn.
3.4	Collaboration and Analysis		
	• I can do a role play about work with my group.	1Cl.01 Working together: Work positively with others, sharing resources while working independently or with others. 1A.04 Solving problems: Choose a possible solution to an issue from a range of actions.	Innovative and equipped for new and future challenges.
3.5	Communication		
	• I can talk about our workplace.	1Cm.01 Communicating information: Answer questions with relevant information about a given issue. 1Cm.02 Listening and responding: Listen to others in class discussions and respond with simple questions.	Engaged intellectually and socially, ready to make a difference.

Lesson	Learning goals	Learning objectives	Learner Attributes
3.6	Reflection		
	• I can talk about what I learned. • I can say what I did to help my group.	1Rf.01 Personal contribution: Identify personal contribution in the form of an action intended to help achieve a shared outcome. 1Rf.02 Teamwork: Identify an action that someone else contributed to achieve a shared outcome. 1Rf.03 Personal perspectives: Talk about what has been learned during an activity with support. 1Rf.04 Personal learning: Talk about something liked in a particular activity.	Reflective as learners, developing their ability to learn.

4 How can we save water?

Outcome	A 'show and tell' in which learners demonstrate ways of using water carefully.
Challenge(s)	Looking after our world.
Curriculum topic(s)	Water, food and farming; Looking after planet Earth.
UN Sustainable Development Goal	• UN Sustainable Development Goal 6: Ensuring clean water and sanitation is available to all.
UN Rights of the Child	• Article 24: Every child has the right to the best possible health. Governments must provide good quality health care, clean water, nutritious food, a clean environment and education on health and wellbeing so that children can stay healthy. Richer countries must help poorer countries achieve this.
Skills focus for assessment	Analysis: 1A.01, 1A.02, 1A.03, 1A.04

Lesson	Learning goals	Learning objectives	Learner Attributes
4.1	Analysis		
	• I can talk about where we use water at school. • I can talk about what happens when I do things.	1A.01 Identifying perspectives: Say something known about an issue. 1A.02 Interpreting data: Talk about information recorded in pictograms or graphic organisers. 1A.03 Making connections: Talk about simple, personal consequences of own actions. 1A.04 Solving problems: Choose a possible solution to an issue from a range of actions given.	Confident in working with information and ideas – their own and those of others.

Lesson	Learning goals	Learning objectives	Learner Attributes
4.2	Research		
	• I can find out about how people use water. • I can record information in a chart.	**1Rs.03** Conducting research: Begin to participate in simple investigations and ask basic questions to find information and opinions. **1Rs.04** Recording findings: Record information on a given issue in pictograms or simple graphic organisers.	Responsible for themselves, responsive to and respectful of others.
4.3	Evaluation and Research		
	• I can say what I think about saving water.	**1E.02** Evaluating perspectives and arguments: State an opinion about a given issue. **1Rs.02** Information skills: Talk about information on a given issue in sources provided.	Engaged intellectually and socially, ready to make a difference.
4.4	Collaboration and Communication		
	• I can work with my group to ask and answer questions about saving water.	**1Cl.01** Working together: Work positively with others, sharing resources while working independently or with others. **1Cm.01** Communicating information: Answer questions with relevant information about a given issue. **1Cm.02** Listening and responding: Listen to others in class discussions and respond with simple questions.	Innovative and equipped for new and future challenges.
4.5	Communication		
	• I can tell other people about using water carefully.	**1Cm.01** Communicating information: Answer questions with relevant information about a given issue. **1Cm.02** Listening and responding: Listen to others in class discussions and respond with simple questions.	Engaged intellectually and socially, ready to make a difference.
4.6	Reflection		
	• I can talk about what I learned. • I can talk about how somebody helped me.	**1Rf.02** Teamwork: Identify an action that someone else contributed to achieve a shared outcome. **1Rf.03** Personal perspectives: Talk about what has been learned during an activity with support.	Reflective as learners, developing their ability to learn. Engaged intellectually and socially, ready to make a difference.

Approaches to teaching Cambridge Primary Global Perspectives

How the projects are structured

Each of the four projects in the Learner's Skills Book is based on a learning journey. The Learner's Skills Book contains four projects that are supported by the guidance and teaching ideas in this Teacher's Resource. Each learning journey leads to a practical action for the learners to complete together as part of a team. Each learning journey is based on one or more of the topics suggested in the curriculum framework. This provides the focus question for each project.

Project 1 is designed to be an age-appropriate introduction to project work. It is based on a theme (families and what we learn from them) that builds directly on the experiences of young children. From Project 2 onwards, the skills are developed in a sequence so that learners focus in turn on each of the skills of Analysis, Research, Evaluation, Collaboration, Communication and Reflection. Each project presents the learners with a focus question or topic. Each project builds to a practical outcome – the learners work towards a way of sharing their understanding in response to this question or topic.

How the projects build on each other

The projects build on each other following a 'spiral' model. This model provides a coherent structure for the whole year's work.

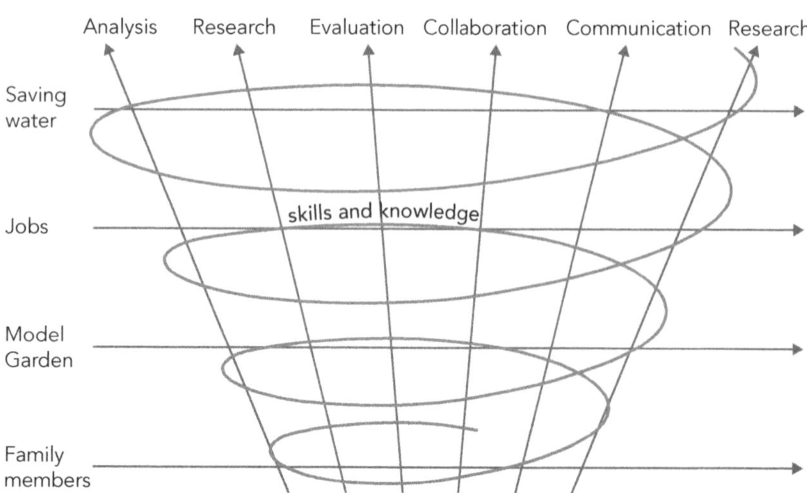

The skills (which are set out in the curriculum) are represented by the upward arrows. The different projects set out in these materials are represented by the horizontal lines. As learners experience the different projects over the course of the year, they apply their skills and understanding in different contexts. The skills taught in each unit are visited and then revisited in a continuous teaching and learning process. This process is represented by the spiral. You will see that the skills reinforce each other with each repetition in a strong teaching and learning structure.

Learners repeatedly follow a similar project structure through a series of relevant topics. Repeated use of skills entrenches them as habits of mind. Repeated journeys will allow them to build gradual independence. The focus on globally relevant but child-focused topics during each project will help learners begin to sort ideas for themselves and understand their world. At each stage, we will help you to help your learners reflect on their achievements and the progress that they have made.

Assessment

Formative assessment

Strategies are provided in each lesson to help you assess learners' attainment accurately against the benchmarks provided in the curriculum framework. We suggest a range of formative assessment strategies to help you adapt your teaching within lessons in light of learners' responses. Example answers are also given. We fully recognise that the learners you are teaching will each begin the projects we set out from different starting points. Their existing knowledge, skills and understanding will vary.

Some have skills that are more or less in line with the sequence of objectives as they are set out in the curriculum framework. Some will already have these skills or will pick them up rapidly. Some may need additional support in order to do so. Listening closely to your learners or reading their written responses as each lesson progresses will help you to adapt your teaching and make sure that the level of challenge is right for each of them across the projects.

Learners working towards learning objectives

You may find that some of your learners do not progress as quickly. They can still use the materials but they will benefit from additional support. Support strategies for them are set out in the differentiation section for each activity. You should monitor their progress closely. Are they demonstrating that their skills are moving more in line with learning objectives in the activities and lessons that follow?

When they do make progress, the level of challenge is clearly appropriate. The support strategies will no longer be necessary on such a regular basis. If they still do not make progress – even with the task broken down into more manageable steps as suggested in the differentiation sections – seek guidance from specialist colleagues. They will be able to suggest further appropriate strategies to meet those learners' individual needs.

Learners working in line with learning objectives

Depending on thir level of prior attainment, you are likely to find that some of your learners make progress in line with learning objectives for this stage as set out in the curriculum framework. Where this is the case, it is also likely that they will be able to access the activities set out without significant additional support. You should still continue to monitor their progress to check that they are still meeting the learning objectives. The learning goals in each section will help you to do this.

If some learners are not successfully applying their understanding in the later activities and projects, they will need to be targeted to receive the additional support strategies. If learners can successfully transfer their skills from a completed project to a new project, they will benefit from the challenge activities suggested. These learners can move to independent learning sooner. They will need less scaffolding and modelling of the skills than before.

Learners working beyond learning objectives for this stage

You may find that some of your learners are working at a level of understanding that is beyond the learning objectives that are set out in the framework for this stage. These learners will certainly benefit from the extra challenge strategies set out. They will not need as much scaffolding and modelling from you. They can begin working independently sooner. Try to ensure that these learners are targeted to receive the extra challenge strategies on a consistent basis. Monitor them closely and look for evidence that they are continuing to be challenged appropriately. Can they still apply their skills at the same level in new contexts? If so, continue to steer them towards the challenge differentiation tasks.

Some exceptional learners will find even some of the challenge activities are not challenging enough. For these learners, look at curriculum framework learning objectives for the later stages. Plan activities to support their learning based on these higher expectations. Look at the materials published for older learners. Seek guidance from specialist colleagues and colleagues who teach older learners. Find out what further strategies they provide that might be appropriate to your learners' individual needs.

Cambridge students understand themselves as learners. They are concerned with the processes as well as the products of their learning and develop the awareness and strategies to be lifelong learners.

Cambridge learning attributes

Skills in self-assessment are an important component of understanding the process of learning. Our materials help you to develop this skill with the learners by setting out a series of 'I can' statements at the start of each lesson. These are designed to be shared with the learners. The 'I can' statements provide learners with clear and easily understood criteria against which they can judge how their skills have developed over the course of each lesson.

The following self-assessment scaffolding can be used to structure learner engagement during reflection activities, and is referenced in the teaching notes that support reflective learning activities. Next to each 'I can' statement are two icons: ☺ and ☹. A learner can use the ☹ icon if they judge that they still need additional support to demonstrate this skill. A learner can use the ☺ icon if they judge that they can demonstrate this skill independently. These statements can be used throughout the lesson to give your learners verbal (and also, where appropriate, written) feedback while they work on the activities.

Learners have a tendency to be harsh in their self-assessment. Of course, as each individual learner self-assesses a range of skills, accuracy will vary enormously. A short space is allocated so that you can give your perspective on learners' next steps – or indicate if there are any 'gap tasks' where appropriate. In this way, learners can be encouraged to respond to your feedback – reflecting on what they have achieved and where to go next in their learning.

Each lesson contains a plenary session. This provides you with a structured opportunity to share examples of learners' responses that meet the criteria for the lesson and for learners to reflect on their own progress during the course of the lesson. There is a space for you to give your own assessment of each learner's progress. It may be the case that a learner is harsh in their self-assessment. This can frequently be the case when they are new to the process. If so, look for opportunities to discuss with them how their work meets the criteria.

Less frequently, learners are over-generous in their self-assessment. A common cause of over-generous self-assessment is underestimating what is required. When this happens, look for opportunities to discuss 'what a good one looks like' and talk about how to break down the task into a series of steps that enable the criteria to be confidently demonstrated.

Throughout the Teacher's Resource, suggested answers are provided to aid these discussions. The use of the icons is designed to form part of a range of appropriate formative assessment strategies. They provide an opportunity for two-way communication to help teachers adapt subsequent teaching within lessons to take into account learners' responses.

Recording learners' progress

Maintaining accurate records of your learners' progress will help you to ensure you set them appropriately challenging targets.

Examples of attainment are provided in each project to help you to assess progress regularly and accurately. We hope that these examples will help you to discuss your learners' progress in each of the skills with them so they can gain a better understanding of how well they have done and what they need to do to improve.

In each unit, one or more specific skills are targeted for a closer focus. All skills are developed in each of the projects, so they could be assessed in any of them, but to ensure the process of assessment remains manageable, specific learning objectives are selected for more focused assessment within each of the four projects. See the table on page xxvii, which shows where each of the learning objectives is assessed.

The frequency of opportunities to monitor learners' progress increases through the projects in this book. The approach to monitoring learners' progress taken is that children of this age are likely to give a more accurate demonstration of the level of their attainment if the process of teaching and learning is as normal as possible. There are no tests. Instead, indicative responses at different levels are provided.

A downloadable for each project is available for your record keeping. The sheet will give you indicative responses at different levels. These will help teachers decide whether children are working towards, in line with or beyond the learning objectives for this stage. As well as providing a reference point for the ongoing assessment of children's progress these sheets can also be discussed with the colleague who will be teaching the class in the academic year that follows. This will help to ensure they can adapt their teaching to the children's level of prior attainment.

An example is provided in the following table:

	Learners working towards learning objectives for this stage will:	Learners working in line with learning objectives for this stage will:	Learners working beyond learning objectives may in addition:
Evaluating perspectives and arguments	State a fact about a given topic or an opinion linked to the topic.	State an opinion about a given issue.	Express an opinion about a given issue, giving reasons for opinion.
Suggested evidence to support this assessment from this project	Talk about a feature that is found in gardens. For example, 'This garden has got a pond.' State an opinion linked to the topic (not the issue): 'I like birds.' Answer questions about other learners' opinions. Q: 'What would Marcus like?' A: 'Fruit' State a fact about their model: 'We made a bench.' State a fact about another group's model: 'This [model] is a green garden.'	Talk about a garden they like: 'I like my uncle's garden. I play cricket.' Talk about other learners' opinions: 'Marcus would like to pick fruit. I would too.' Name a feature that they would like to see in a school garden and say what they feel about it: 'It is nice to do work outside. We can put a chair under the tree.' Describe a feature that they have put in their school garden model and say what they feel about it: 'We have made a swing. It is so nice.'	Talk about a garden they like and say why: 'My uncle's garden is so good for cricket. The grass is flat.' Talk about other learners' opinions giving reasons: 'Marcus would like to pick fruit. I would too, because I pick plums. They are so nice when you get them from the tree.' Give more than one reason in support of their opinion about why a particular feature would be a good idea: 'It is nice to read outside – sometimes the birds come. Inside it is hot. We can sit in the shade outside. We need a nice chair under the tree.' Describe a feature that they have put in their school garden model and say what they feel about it and why: 'We have made a swing. It is so nice. Look! It moves.'

Cross-curricular links and themes

The resources give you suggestions about how you can integrate each project with theme-based learning – for example, plants, animals and nature in the world around us.

There is information about how each project builds understanding relevant to the UN Sustainable Development Goals. For example, Sustainable Development Goal 2: End hunger, achieve food security and improved nutrition and promote sustainable agriculture.

There are also suggestions about how each project can be used to help learners understand their rights as set out in UN conventions – for example, UN Right of the Child 12: Children have the right to give their opinions freely on issues that affect them. Adults should listen and take children seriously.

Information is provided about how each project can be used to develop learners' understanding in other subjects and/or apply this knowledge/understanding. This is given across a range of subjects. For example:

In this project, learners have the opportunity to develop their **scientific** understanding by:

- exploring ways that different animals and plants inhabit local environments
- considering what plants need to grow
- considering how food grown in gardens can contribute to a healthy diet.

At the end of each project, there is advice on Taking it further. This contains ideas on how to extend learners' understanding of the issues and apply their newly acquired skills in different ways.

Teaching Cambridge Primary Global Perspectives within the wider curriculum

Teachers of young children will rightly want to know about the place of the discipline within the wider curriculum. How can we make Cambridge Primary Global Perspectives 'fit' within an extremely busy school day/week/term/year? How does the study of Cambridge Primary Global Perspectives contribute to the development of the 'whole child'?

Cambridge Primary Global Perspectives takes as its focus issues that are faced by the whole of humanity. Of course, the impact and nature of these issues vary. Exploring important issues with learners who are in the process of understanding the world around them provides a wealth of opportunities to ask questions. What problems present themselves in the world that they see? What possible solutions can we imagine and put in place? In the process of exploring these ideas, learners will develop important and transferable knowledge, understanding and skills.

Learners will have the opportunity to apply knowledge, understanding and skills from subjects such as English, Maths, Science and Technology in new ways. Every project set out in this guide will provide a rich context for purposeful speaking, listening, reading and writing. This process of exchange will be still further enriched where schools are able to make links with other schools in contrasting localities and explore some of the same questions in parallel. See 'Developing a global perspective' on page xxxi for further guidance.

A note of caution is necessary. The teaching of generalised 'topics' can result in a fragmented approach at the cost of meaningful development in skills. Unfortunately, the repetition of broad topics such as 'Homes' year after year has historically led to children unnecessarily going over the same ground. Cambridge Primary Global Perspectives should be considered as an integral part of long-term plans for curriculum continuity and progression. This is a whole-school issue. Cambridge Primary Global Perspectives works best as part of a rich, balanced curriculum.

In each chapter of the Teacher's Resource, we identify how skills from other disciplines can be meaningfully applied in Cambridge Primary Global Perspectives-focused learning. Where appropriate, we explore English, maths, science, the humanities, technology and creative subjects as well as physical education.

The cross-curricular links provided at the beginning of each chapter of this Teacher's Resource show how links can be made between the Cambridge Primary Global Perspectives projects and different subjects across the curriculum. You may also want to think about how each project can fit into a broader theme. The mind map below shows how the Cambridge Primary Global Perspectives project 'What kind of garden would be best?' could be used as a context for developing skills in a number of subject areas. (Note that this diagram is not exhaustive in displaying the cross-curricular links that could be made with this project.)

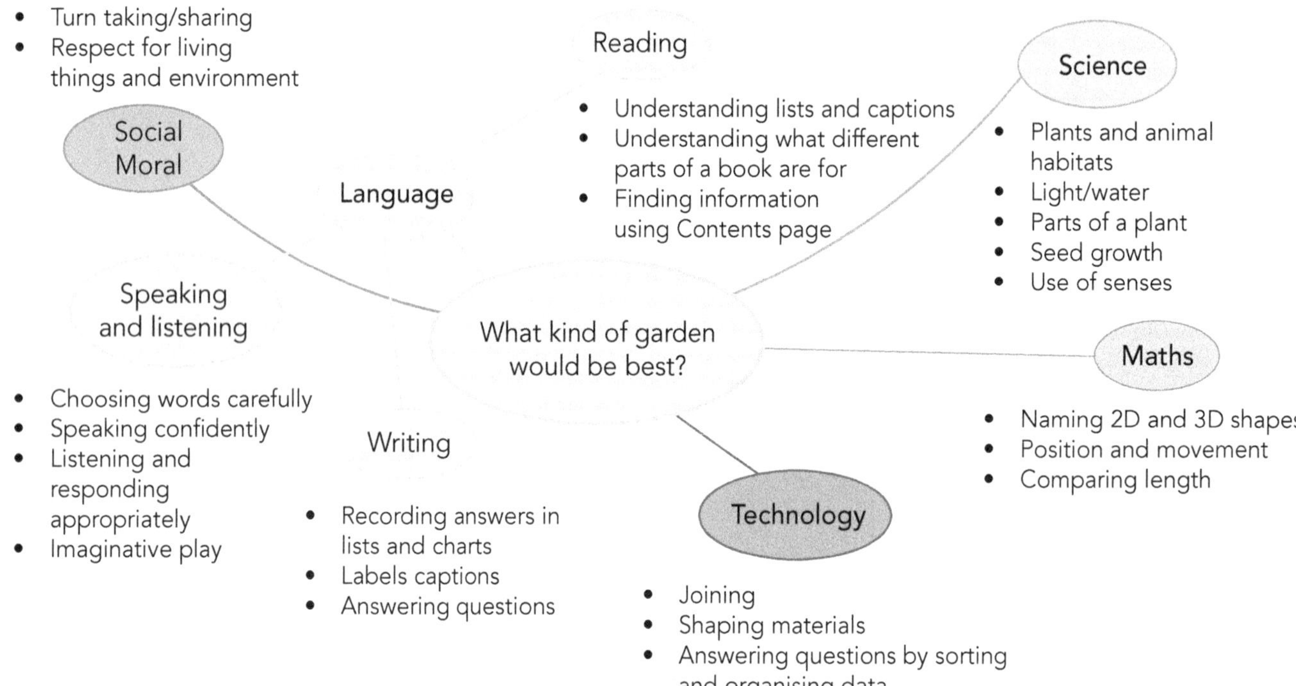

Teaching Cambridge Primary Global Perspectives when English is not the learners' first language

Cambridge Primary Global Perspectives can form a valuable component of a curriculum that is appropriate, relevant and engaging for a diverse school community. Good teaching in Cambridge Primary Global Perspectives is like good teaching in all subjects – learners will succeed when teaching is pitched at the right cognitive level. This is the case regardless of the learners' first language. The role of the teacher in modelling the language that is appropriate for Cambridge Primary Global Perspectives is of central importance.

Different schools will have different perspectives on the use of first language, and you should always teach Global Perspectives in a way that is consistent with your school's overall policy for developing children's language skills.

Is it essential to use English at all times in Cambridge Primary Global Perspective classrooms? This is not necessarily the case. Learners might find their first language more appropriate to activate their prior understanding – much of which will have been acquired in their first language. Our materials scaffold understanding, but the ideas are supposed to be challenging. When working through complex ideas, it can be appropriate to use your first language to do so initially. Translating into and from your first language can reinforce ideas. Learners who share a first language can develop ideas as talk partners, using their first language initially. Bilingual dictionaries could well be useful – especially with the words in the glossary.

However, learners will need to use English in Cambridge Primary Global Perspectives to develop fluency. If they are getting ready to write in English it is a good idea to rehearse the content orally in English first. If you are planning a presentation in English, then they will need to be encouraged to take risks with and gain confidence in their spoken English before they speak to an audience.

To help you guide all learners, in each section the goals are specified clearly. The 'Answers and formative assessment' sections provide suggestions on how you can judge if learners' responses show that they have grasped the aim. The differentiation section sets out ways in which learners can be supported further to demonstrate the focus skill. You will also have your own formative assessment of the level of language your learners are comfortable working with. This will enable you to select an appropriate pathway through each section and provide the right level of scaffolding to support their understanding – or to extend it further.

Some additional ways in which you can make use of our resources to help your learners develop their language skills are set out below:

- **Scaffolded skills development** – Structured, purposeful learning that helps learners make sense of the world benefits all learners. Learners whose first language is not English particularly benefit from regular opportunities to activate their prior understanding. Our Starter Activities make sure that your learners have time to think about and process what they already know before taking on new ideas. The way that skills are built up is always scaffolded in our materials.

  For example, in the project 'What kind of garden would be best?', the third lesson asks 'Where can I find more facts and ideas?' Learners are asked to look at different sources and say if they would be useful. This requires them to consider relevance. The cognitive demand here is at a challenging level – but our friendly characters are on hand in the Learner's Skills Book to provide support.

- **Characters** – The use of characters in the book is designed to model not just Global Perspectives skills but the language processes that support them. The needs of learners whose first language is not English underpins the support provided. For example, one of the characters is deciding whether or not a book is useful for their research. They make the following observation:

  Zara: This is not a good source because it hasn't got any ideas about gardens!

  The amount of additional scaffolding required for your learners to make effective use of this modelling to provide their own answers will depend on their language proficiency. One possible strategy is to use the model text provided in the skills book to set up a sentence framework. These frameworks can scaffold how to make an appropriate response for learners who are new to English.

<table>
<tr><td rowspan="4">This</td><td rowspan="2">is</td><td rowspan="2">a very good source</td><td>it has got plenty of</td><td rowspan="4">ideas about gardens</td></tr>
<tr><td>it has got some</td></tr>
<tr><td rowspan="2">is not</td><td rowspan="2">a good source because</td><td>it has not got many</td></tr>
<tr><td>it has not got any</td></tr>
</table>

  Let's look at another example. Later in the unit, learners are asked to tell their partner what kind of garden they would like and why. The Learner's Skills Book contains the following comment:

  Arun: I would like a seat and some sunflowers. Children can sit and watch the birds eating the sunflower seeds.

  The following scaffold structure can be used to guide learners' responses when they consider the kind of garden they would like to see, and includes blank spaces for additional suggestions from learners.

I would like	a seat	and	some sunflowers.	Children	can	sit	and	watch the birds	eating the sunflower seeds	.
	a pond	under	some fish.	Parents		stand		watch the fish	swimming in the water	
	some grass	in	wind chimes.			lie	or	listen to the chimes	with a ball	
	a tree	with	a tree.	Older people		relax		run	and have fun	
			space to play.			play		read a book	in the shade	

Discussing the characters' examples will help your learners to identify and explain issues that are part of their own experience. This modelling approach has been adopted throughout our materials, and feedback from teachers who have used it strongly suggests that learners find the examples extremely helpful in supporting their understanding.

- **Vocabulary** – Using our Learner's Skills Book will help you understand what vocabulary will be needed in the lesson and prepare appropriately. Key terms are picked out in the text and given in an extensive glossary. It is likely that there will at times be additional terms that are unfamiliar. These can be clarified in line with your school policy – for example, by providing word mats or displays that enable them to quickly access definitions of key vocabulary.
- **Planned talk** – The Teacher's Resource sets out regular opportunities for planned talk. This is often through the use of talk partners, and opportunities for pair talk are regularly set out in the Learner's Skill's Book. This is particularly useful for learners whose first language is not English so that they have plenty of opportunities to rehearse the use of appropriate language before they speak to a larger audience.
- **Oral rehearsal** – Oral rehearsal prior to any writing is a consistent approach that we have adopted.
- **Collaborative learning** – Cambridge Primary Global Perspectives provides a rich context for the use of collaborative learning. Group work is regularly planned for – but drama, group presentations and a range of other strategies that promote effective language development have also been suggested. We believe that the study of Cambridge Primary Global Perspectives can form part of your range of innovative strategies that establish a safe and stimulating environment for all learners. This includes learners whose first language is not English. The emphasis on collaborative work will help you to build relationships which are rooted in mutual respect. Collaborative work on practical tasks is a rich context for language acquisition and motivates and inspires all learners to engage with the issues and develop their skills.
- **Features of spoken language** – Even learners who have gained a good level of proficiency in spoken English can need additional support to understand what kind of language is appropriate in different contexts. Global Perspectives is no different to other learning contexts in this respect. Supporting ideas effectively with evidence and reasoning is a central focus of learning in Global Perspectives. Doing so does require learners to structure their responses to the tasks in specific ways.

While our materials do not deal explicitly with grammar structures, learners whose first language is not English will benefit especially from the structured support provided in a series of modelled conversations in the downloadable materials. In the following example, the characters are discussing what they would like to see in a garden:

What questions can we ask?

Sofia: So, what do you think?
Arun: About the garden for the school?
Sofia: Yes.

Arun: I would like butterflies to come.
Marcus: I would like fruit to pick. That would be so nice.
Zara: I would like a bug hotel.
Sofia: What is a bug hotel?
Zara: You put lots of wood and sticks. The bugs come to live inside.
Sofia: Arun, how do you get butterflies to come?
Arun: You need special flowers.

Q1: What are the children talking about?
A1: A school garden.
Q2: What is Arun's idea.
A2: Arun wants to grow flowers so butterflies will come.
Q3: What is Marcus's idea?
A3: Marcus wants to grow fruit to eat.
Q4: What is Zara's idea?
A4: Zara wants a bug hotel.

Working with parents and care givers

Parents and care givers can potentially play a hugely valuable role as part of a rich curriculum. Actively seeking out different perspectives is of central importance. Learners should be encouraged to ask their parents, care givers and other trusted adults what their perspective is on the issues raised by the materials. Cambridge Primary Global Perspectives provides a range of opportunities for parents and care givers whose first language is not English to play an active role in their children's learning. The diversity of parents' and care givers' experiences is a huge potential asset to the Cambridge Primary Global Perspectives classroom. We hope that you will encourage all learners, regardless of their first language, to talk about the issues that you have discussed in class when they get home in whatever language is most appropriate to this context.

Developing a global perspective

The materials in this course are based on the idea that learners will be developing their own perspective in response to the world that they experience. This process is best understood as a dynamic one. The learners are active participants. As they engage with their immediate surroundings, they develop their personal and local perspective. Their experience is not limited to the personal and local.

There are a number of reasons why this is so. Children live in a world built on global exchange. Our young learners' experience is shaped by much that is globalised. This includes media that they consume. Many of the learners that we teach will have extended families that span continents. Their growing sense of their place in the world will be formed by their understanding of a range of different experiences. In the classroom, they will exchange ideas with others whose experiences are similar to and different from their own. We make sure that they have plenty of opportunities to talk to other learners in a focused way.

Take the example of a learner (A) who is sat opposite another learner (B) on a carpet in a classroom talking about jobs. Learner A has an auntie in a different country. Auntie was talking about her job last night on a family video call. Learner B has one parent who works in a local shop; the second parent travels around the country as part of their work. During this conversation, what perspective is being developed? Is it personal, local, national or global? Well, the answer is, of course, all four.

As teachers, we need to ensure the examples we bring in to the classroom are appropriate. This is fundamental to the process of teaching and learning. These published materials are designed to provide complete coverage of the Cambridge Global Perspectives curriculum. Each project provides a structured approach, providing an integrated learning journey through the skills of Analysis, Research, Evaluation, Collaboration and Reflection. When planning for any specific class, we need to remember that these materials have been written for a global readership. They cannot provide a local perspective. Effective teachers of Cambridge Global Perspectives will work collaboratively to develop their teaching. They will enrich the resources provided by also using local analogies, illustrations, examples, explanations and demonstrations.

The COVID-19 pandemic took away face-to-face collaborative learning with peers. Resourceful teachers who had the necessary technology at their disposal worked to ensure that learning continued to the best of their abilities. This means that we understand the potential (and some of the pitfalls) of remote learning better than ever before. The materials are based on the premise that effective grouping and the use of pair work strategies such as talk partners support the needs of all learners.

Teachers of Cambridge Global Perspectives who are using these materials have the potential to provide their learners with a rich comparative perspective. Working through the projects in partnership with colleagues in a contrasting international context will vastly enrich the experience. There is a wide range of forums available to find suitable partners. What better way could there be for learners to develop a global perspective than to consider the same questions as their peers from a contrasting global context?

The projects in these resources are based on universal human needs: The relationship of people to the natural world, the need for gainful employment, the need for water, family and community learning and shared culture. Human needs are universal. The way that they are met and experienced differs. Learners can benefit immensely by sharing their understanding of their experiences in relation to these universal concerns. Learners working in partnership with international peers can come to an understanding of diversity. Some examples of how curriculum objectives can be enriched in this way are provided in the table below.

For further information on how you can cover global themes in a local context for younger learners, you can watch or listen to the Cambridge University Press Education podcast from March 2021, 'Thinking globally and acting locally. What does that mean for primary children?' The section from 38 minutes until the end is particularly relevant.

Curriculum objective	Developing a local perspective	Developing a global perspective
Analysis		
Say something known about an issue.	Saying something known about the issue as it impacts on the local area.	Comparing something known about the issue as it impacts on the local area with the impacts in a partner school's locality.
Choose a possible solution to an issue from a range of actions given, e.g. what plants could we grow to attract bees?	Choosing a possible solution to an issue from a range of actions given because it is appropriate to a local need, e.g. choose from a range of plants because they a) attract bees and b) grow well locally.	Comparing how possible solutions to the given issue are similar/different because they are appropriate to different local needs. E.g. compare: plants, how they grow, when where to plant them, how many bees come.
Communication		
Answer questions with relevant information about a given issue.	Answering a question with relevant local information about a given issue.	Comparing answers to the same question based on different local information about a given issue.

Curriculum objective	Developing a local perspective	Developing a global perspective
Listen to others in class discussions and respond with simple questions.	Listening to others in class discussions about their experience of the local area and responding with simple questions.	Listening to a recording of an international peer talking about their experience in their local area and responding with simple questions.
Evaluation		
State an opinion about a given issue.	Stating an opinion about a given issue based on their experience in their own local area.	Comparing their own opinion about a given issue based on their experience in their own local area with an opinion on the same issue from an international peer.

Transferring your skills as a teacher

Cambridge Primary Global Perspectives is an interdisciplinary programme. Learners do not learn facts, instead they build up a range of skills. As we have seen, the key skills of Analysis, Research, Evaluation, Communication, Collaboration and Reflection are taught through a series of projects. These build good learners. They are also skills that are central to good teaching. Our feedback shows that colleagues across the world have welcomed the priorities of our Cambridge Primary Global Perspectives resources. Specifically, they have commented on the scope for active learning, metacognition, reflective learning and integrating real-world local and global issues. Colleagues have welcomed our materials for many reasons.

- Engaging with global issues and exploring their relevance locally helps learners to aim high. Research is based in the real world. Collaboration is focused on making a positive change. Honest reflection on the process builds trust between learners.
- The regular opportunities to reflect on progress helps to build self-motivated learners. Tackling tangible local issues with a view to making a positive change generates enthusiasm for learning. Teachers develop effectiveness through being alert to local examples and this stimulates, and capture their learners' interest. Our materials have helped teachers to help learners broaden and deepen the contributions they make.
- Growing young global citizens enhances the life and ethos of the school as well as of the wider community it serves.
- Engaging methods to help learners reflect on their own progress. Colleagues use this to build their knowledge of learners' prior attainment across the curriculum. They welcome the regular and systematic progress checks in Cambridge Primary Global Perspectives skills provided in our resources.
- The scaffolding that our materials provide ensures that cognitive load is managed appropriately. This helps ensure that, over time, learners become more independent.
- The high expectations of the Cambridge Primary Global Perspectives framework, together with the scaffolding in the materials, will enhance effective colleagues' strategies for maintaining a stimulating learning environment. They welcome the emphasis on high levels of engagement, collaboration and cooperation in structured group tasks.

Finally, a global community of Cambridge Global Perspectives teachers enjoy opportunities to build professional relationships. They welcome opportunities to work collaboratively with international colleagues. A growing number of Cambridge Global Perspectives teachers are taking advantage of opportunities provided by Cambridge International to develop their practice through a wide range of continuing professional development activities and courses. Why not join them?

Approaches to teaching and learning

The following are the teaching approaches underpinning our course content and how we understand and define them.

Active learning

Active learning is a teaching approach that places student learning at its centre. It focuses on how students learn, not just on what they learn. We, as teachers, need to encourage learners to 'think hard', rather than passively receive information. Active learning encourages learners to take responsibility for their learning and supports them in becoming independent and confident learners in school and beyond.

Assessment for learning

Assessment for Learning (AfL) is a teaching approach that generates feedback which can be used to improve learners' performance. Learners become more involved in the learning process and, from this, gain confidence in what they are expected to learn and to what standard. We, as teachers, gain insights into a learner's level of understanding of a particular concept or topic, which helps to inform how we support their progression.

Differentiation

Differentiation is usually presented as a teaching approach where teachers think of learners as individuals and learning as a personalised process. Whilst precise definitions can vary, typically the core aim of differentiation is viewed as ensuring that all learners make progress towards their learning intentions. It is about using different approaches and appreciating the differences in learners to help them make progress. Teachers therefore need to be responsive, and willing and able to adapt their teaching to meet the needs of their learners.

Language awareness

For many learners, English is an additional language. It might be their second or perhaps their third language. Depending on the school context, students might be learning all or just some of their subjects through English.

For all learners, regardless of whether they are learning through their first language or an additional language, language is a vehicle for learning. It is through language that students access the learning intentions of the lesson and communicate their ideas. It is our responsibility, as teachers, to ensure that language doesn't present a barrier to learning.

Metacognition

Metacognition describes the processes involved when learners plan, monitor, evaluate and make changes to their own learning behaviours. These processes help learners to think about their own learning more explicitly and ensure that they are able to meet a learning goal that they have identified themselves or that we, as teachers, have set.

Skills for life

How do we prepare learners to succeed in a fast-changing world? To collaborate with people from around the globe? To create innovation as technology increasingly takes over routine work? To use advanced thinking skills in the face of more complex challenges? To show resilience in the face of constant change? At Cambridge, we are responding to educators who have asked for a way to understand how all these different approaches to life skills and competencies relate to their teaching. We have grouped these skills into six main Areas of Competency that can be incorporated into teaching, and have examined the different stages of the learning journey and how these competencies vary across each stage.

These six key areas are:

- Creativity – finding new ways of doing things, and solutions to problems
- Collaboration – the ability to work well with others
- Communication – speaking and presenting confidently and participating effectively in meetings
- Critical thinking – evaluating what is heard or read, and linking ideas constructively
- Learning to learn – developing the skills to learn more effectively
- Social responsibilities – contributing to social groups, and being able to talk to and work with people from other cultures.

Cambridge learner and teacher attributes

This course helps develop the following Cambridge learner and teacher attributes.

Cambridge learners	Cambridge teachers
Confident in working with information and ideas – their own and those of others.	Confident in teaching their subject and engaging each student in learning.
Responsible for themselves, responsive to and respectful of others.	Responsible for themselves, responsive to and respectful of others.
Reflective as learners, developing their ability to learn.	Reflective as learners themselves, developing their practice.
Innovative and equipped for new and future challenges.	Innovative and equipped for new and future challenges.
Engaged intellectually and socially, ready to make a difference.	Engaged intellectually, professionally and socially, ready to make a difference.

Reproduced from Developing the Cambridge learner attributes *with permission from Cambridge Assessment International Education.*

More information about these approaches to teaching and learning is available to download from Cambridge GO.

Glossary of terms

Formative assessment refers to assessment that takes place during the learning process. This is used during the lesson to check progress. Formative assessment strategies can take a variety of forms. Effective formative assessment ensures that all learners receive learning activities that are at an appropriate level of challenge. Formative assessment also ensures that accurate and regular feedback can be given to each learner on how they are progressing and what their next steps should be.

The term **scaffolding** refers to structured help for a child so that they can go on to solve a problem, carry out a task, or achieve a goal independently. This process involves the gradual removal of additional help. Learners with lower prior attainment will need more support before they can achieve success in an activity. Learners with higher prior attainment will need less support before they can successfully complete the activity for themselves.

Think–Pair–Share is a strategy to help learners to generate their own ideas. It builds confidence. There are three steps:

- **Think** – Ask learners a question and give them time to think for themselves. Sometimes it can be useful to provide some key vocabulary.
- **Pair** – Learners pair up to tell a partner their ideas, focusing on the question. This allows learners the chance to practise their answer and develop their ideas further in discussion.
- **Share** – Learners share the ideas that they have come up with with the class.

Junk modelling refers to creating new things from common, discarded, non-toxic items. Modelling helps learners to develop their imagination and creative abilities. Using discarded items to represent their own ideas challenges them to problem solve.

Imaginative play refers to make-believe games and role play during which learners guide their own learning and explore their own ideas.

Playing (in costume in a role-play area or with play people in a model) can be done alone or with others. It provides an important means for learners to understand their world.

Learners can use imaginative play to explore different people's perspectives based upon things that they have seen people do in their own experience.

Using a **working wall** is a strategy to make sure classroom display boards are used effectively as a resource to support learning. Often, teachers use a working wall to show progress along a learning journey. Start and end points of a project are clearly identified so that learners (and teachers) can understand (and demonstrate) how the learning at any given point in the project fits in to the overall aims and contributes to identified outcomes. Sometimes this can initially take the form of a series of questions that will be explored during the course of the project.

Continuous provision describes a way of organising a classroom into specific areas. This way of organising the classroom space is most commonly used with younger learners and involves the provision of specific resources that learners can make use of – either alongside a facilitating adult or independently. Effective continuous provision enables teachers to harness imaginative play as part of the process of teaching and learning. Topic-themed resources, such as appropriate writing materials, paper, topic-focused vocabulary displays and stimulating images, as well as books, are introduced into areas of continuous provision so that specific concepts can be explored and identified skills can be developed.

> 1 What can families teach us?

Introduction

In this project, learners explore what they can learn from older family members, drawing on their life experience and knowledge of family celebrations, stories or games. At the end of the project, the learners create a display to summarise their findings, and they share what they have found out through talking, writing or drawing, according to their preference.

To start with, learners consider who is in their family, and the different names that these family members are called by. They then think about what these family members have taught them. As they progress through this project, learners gather information from older family members, interviewing an older person to find details about their childhood (Lesson 3 Research). They then compare the information shared by their classmates, and compare their own lives with the lives of the older members of their family when they were children (Lessons 4 and 5 Analysis). All through the project, the learners respond to questions asked by the teacher, participate in discussions and present a display to share what they have learned from older family members (Communication).

Towards the end of the project, the learners have the opportunity to reflect on what they have learned from older members of the family, how their lives are different and what they have learned and enjoyed while doing this project; later, they reflect on their own learning in the project and in particular on what they did or did not enjoy doing (Lessons 5 and 6 Reflection). Learners also have the opportunity, throughout, to collaborate with their partners when they share information on what they call older family members, or on the things that they have learned from older members of the family (Collaboration). (At the end of the interview, learners discuss the process of the interview and evaluate whether an interview is a reliable source for information).

As learners advance through the project, they will mainly have opportunities to develop their *personal perspective* when they share their findings and discover the personal perspectives of their classmates. The perspectives of learners can be broadened to the *global perspective* when they read about the experiences of other learners and their family members who live in different parts of the world from the stories, information and the audio recording shared in the Learner's Skills Book.

It is useful for teachers to acknowledge that the learners' experiences of families can be varied and diverse. Teachers must ensure that all learners feel comfortable to share about their families. The vocabulary used by the teacher to talk about family members and relationships must be sensitive to differences and help learners to welcome and respect the heterogeneous nature of families. At all times, the teacher must help learners to identify older members who are trusted and play a role in contributing to their lives, growth and development.

The project opens up extensive opportunities for input from the learners' families or care givers, and this will obviously be easier if you already have close, cooperative links with them. In the project, you will need to arrange a class visit from a grandparent (ideally) or another older person (or even a school staff member) who is willing to be interviewed about their earlier life. In addition, you will need to ask for help from the parents/care givers in three ways:

- Talking to the learners about who is in their family and where they live
- Allowing one family member to be 'interviewed', answering the learners' (prepared) questions about their childhood
- Providing a suitable story, anecdote, game, song or similar from their own childhood, that the learners could then share with the class.

You will need to be flexible in planning the project to take account of the diverse nature of (and varying levels of) input from the families.

Cross-curricular links and themes.

This project lends itself particularly well to integration with theme-based learning on the family, including the understanding of the importance of love, security and stability.

The theme of families and learning developed throughout this project builds understanding relevant to the UN Sustainable Development Goal 4: Ensure inclusive and equitable quality education and promote lifelong learning opportunities for all. This means ensuring access to quality education and considering the importance of effective home–school partnerships to this aim. Building understanding of what they learn from their home and community can be used to develop learner's understanding that they have a number of rights under the UN Convention on the Rights of the Child. As teachers, being aware of these rights helps us to understand the significant role that families and other adults can play in the life of a learner.

- Article 5: You have the right to be given guidance by your parents and family.
- Article 9: You have the right to live with your parents, unless it is bad for you.
- Article 18: You have the right to be brought up by your parents, if possible.

Learners have opportunities to apply their knowledge and understanding of, and skills in:	
Reading skills	• Reading and listening to a range of family-themed books, drawing on background information and vocabulary provided • Making links from their reading to their own experiences of sharing stories with family members • Demonstrating their understanding of explicit meaning in text provided about the experiences and expertise of older people.
Writing skills	• Selecting and developing content appropriate to conveying their understanding of family stories, games, festivals or particular expertise
Speaking and listening skills	• Listening to others (learners and adults) and responding appropriately • Asking and listening carefully to questions • Listening to and giving instructions
Before beginning work on this project, it would be helpful if learners have knowledge of or have had previous experience of:	
• Who their family members are, where they are located and the roles they play within the family • Being able to identify who their 'trusted adults' are both within their family and wider circles • Reading simple words using phonic and sight word knowledge • Writing words and simple sentences (with assistance if required) • Using drawing to illustrate their thoughts and ideas.	
Assessment focus	
The focus skill for this project is Communication. The following downloadables will support you with assessing learners' attainment against the curriculum framework: • Downloadable 1.6 (Assessment guidance sheet: Communication) • Downloadable 1.7 (Assessment record sheet: Communication) For a general introduction to the approach to assessment in this course, see page xxiii.	

Getting started

Good for: Setting the tone of the project; helping learners to identify relationships within their own family by looking at examples within pictures of other people's families; recapitulating the terms used to refer to family members.

Activity:

1 Do this activity as a class. Display or draw attention to the three 'photographs' (Learner's Skills Book page 10–11) and ask learners to look at them in turn. Introduce the four characters – Zara, Sofia, Arun and Marcus – explaining that the learners will meet these characters a lot throughout the book. Ask who the other people in each photo might be. Why do they think so? Support learners as necessary with words that describe relationships in a family: father, mother, grandfather, grandmother, aunt, uncle, cousin and so on.

   Ask the learners what the people in each picture are doing. When discussing the 'photos' of Sofia and Marcus's families, bring out the theme of older people teaching younger people by asking appropriate questions. With regard to Sofia's family, you might ask: *What is Grandpa doing? What is Sofia doing? Do you think she knows how to cook? How is she learning to cook?* For Marcus's family, you could ask: *What is Marcus doing? What do you think Grandma is saying to Marcus? Do your family show you how to do things?*

2 Broaden the discussion to talk more generally about the kinds of things learners like doing at home with their own family or care givers.

Answers: This will depend on the learner's prior experience and their interests. It is useful for the rest of the project to draw out some of the following:

- Families vary greatly. We cannot assume that other people's families will be like ours.
- We can learn a lot of things by spending time with the older people around us.

Differentiation:

Give support by showing more pictures either from books or on slides to give learners more visual input in terms of different kinds of families. You can also refer to familiar stories, or stories that the learners have encountered in either their textbooks, library books or similar. Pictures that show families from different parts of the world can help learners to talk and share ideas about all kinds of families from all types of backgrounds and geographical locations.

1.1 Who is in my family?

LEARNING OBJECTIVES: ANALYSIS

1A.01 Identifying perspectives: Say something known about an issue

1A.02 Interpreting data: Talk about information recorded in pictograms or graphic organisers

ADDITIONAL LEARNING OBJECTIVES

1Rs.01 Constructing research questions: Ask basic questions about a given issue

LEARNING GOALS

- I can say who is in my family.
- I can find out if we all use the same names for family members.

LEARNING ATTRIBUTES

This lesson gives learners the opportunity to be:

- Confident in working with information and ideas – their own and those of others.

Resources needed

Learners to bring a photograph or a drawing of their family members

Learner's Skills Book pages 12–15

Downloadable 1.1 (photos of different kinds of families)

Starter

Good for: Recapping the learning about family relationships from Getting Started to help learners with the activities in this lesson

Activity: Ask learners if they can remember the photos of Arun, Sofia and Marcus's families. Conduct a quick quiz: say the name of the character (Arun, Sofia or Marcus) and learners have to name a member of their family who appeared in the picture. Alternatively, say the name of a family member and learners have to identify whose family photo included that family member. If you think learners will have forgotten, display the pictures again (covering up the labels) as you ask questions such as: *Whose family is this? Whose grandmother is this?* and so on.

Who are my family members?

Good for: Learners to identify members of their own family and begin to recognise that families can be different.

Activity:

1 Remind learners that they have been finding out about the families of Arun, Sofia and Marcus; whose family do they think they will find out about next? (Their own!) Ask them what sort of things they could find out about families. Note down their suggestions and discuss.

Focus attention on the picture of Arun's family. Ask questions to help learners identify who the members of Arun's family are (his sister, his uncle, his father and his mother).

Share pictures (e.g. those on downloadable 1.1) representing different kinds of families (from different backgrounds and geographical areas, if possible) – for example, *small nuclear families, extended families, families where learners live with grandparents or single-parent families*. Ask learners to identify who the people might be in each family.

Discuss with learners that families are different and varied; they can be different in terms of the number of people in the family or which family members they include.

Ask a few learners to say who is in *their* family. Appreciate each learner's contribution.

Ask learners to draw a picture of the family members who live with them (in their book or on a separate sheet of paper). Alternatively – with advance notice – they could bring in a photo from home to stick in their book. They should then write the name of each family member on or just below the picture.

2 Share a personal example of a relative who does not live with you (e.g. my brother doesn't live with us, he lives in...). Ask learners if they have similar examples to share. You could discuss whether the relative lives nearby or far away in a completely different town or even a different country. Tell learners to write the names of some family members who do not live with them. They should also write where those relatives live, if they know. (You could ask them to find out details at home from their parents/care givers and report back in a later lesson). If required, help learners with spellings of the names that they would like to write. Ask learners to share their answers with their partners.

Answers and formative assessment: Each learner's answer will be based on the type of family they come comes from. Check whether learners are able to describe their family and say who the family members are.

Differentiation:

Give support by helping learners with spelling (e.g. telling learners to look for spellings of family relationships from the pictures in Getting Started or writing out the common ones on the board for learners to copy). If learners have specific family names that they would like to include, suggest that they ask for help from their family at home.

Give extra challenge by asking learners to compare their family with Arun's family. Can they identify how their family is similar or different? Which family members are there or not there? Also ask learners to identify who is older than them or younger than them.

What do I call my adult family members?

Good for: Exploring names and different way in which family members are addressed

Activity:

1 Introduce the session by saying that it is time to discover something interesting about our classmates' families.

Encourage learners to read the speech bubbles. Draw attention to and repeat the key words: *Marcus – grandmother – Ada – Nanna, Arun – father – Arjun – Papa*. Ask learners to point in the illustration and speech bubble. To check understanding, ask questions: *What is Marcus's grandmother's name? What does he call her? What is Arun's father's name? What does he call him?*

Give one or two examples (real or invented) based on your own family – for example, *My father's name is Silvio but I call him Dad. My grandmother's name was Maria but I called her Nonna.* Ask some more confident learners to share examples of their own with the class.

Play a quick game: each learner names a family member. They say their given name and follow it by what they call them – for example, *father, Arjun, Papa*. Learners can choose to name any family member. (This way, different family relationships can be considered).

Demonstrate how to record these answers in a very simple table (like the one in the Learner's Skills Book).

Explain to the learners that this is called a table.

Family member	What I call them
Father	Dada

Look together at Marcus and Arun's speech bubbles in the Learner's Skills Book. Ask a learner to add the information about Marcus's family (and another learner to do the same for Arun's family) in the table you created.

Learners complete the table on page 14 in the Learner's Skills and share with their partner one or two more names of family members and what they call them.

2 Ask learners to consider other people who look after them. Encourage learners to talk about babysitters, day-care staff, neighbours and so on. What names do they have for these people? Learners write their own answers in the Learner's Skills Book.

Answers and formative assessment: Answers will depend on each learner's individual family and circumstances. Check whether learners are able to identify and share the name of a family member and explain how they are addressed.

Differentiation:

Give support by helping learners with spelling (e.g. telling learners to look for spellings of family relationships from the pictures in Getting Started or writing out the common ones on the board for learners to copy). If learners have specific family names that they would like to include, suggest that they ask for help from their family at home.

Give extra challenge by asking learners to say why they think we have different ways of addressing our family members. Explore how languages cause us to address family members using different vocabulary.

Do we all have the same names for our family members?

Good for: Identifying differences and similarities in the way in which we address older family members or people.

Activity: Divide learners into small groups of three or four. Tell them it is Listen and Share Time. Remind learners that families can be different, and each person in the group may have different people in their families. Tell learners to talk to the other learners in their group. They should tell them what they have written in their chart.

Learners should listen to each other carefully. Do others in the group use the same or different names for their family members? Tell learners to record their findings in the Learner's Skills Book – they should try to write one family member where everyone in the group uses the same name and one where they have different names. Encourage the learners to help each other by listening carefully and working together.

Look at the 'Did you know?' box together. What names are used for grandmothers where you live? Do learners know any other names that are used for a grandmother, perhaps in other countries that they are familiar with?

Answers: Responses will be individual. Use the diverse responses to reiterate that families can be different and varied.

Differentiation:

Give support by assisting learners with spellings when required. You could show how to do the activity by joining one of the groups and demonstrating what to do for the whole class (using your examples of what you call your family members and comparing your names with theirs).

Give extra challenge by asking learners to compare their charts with another group's, and to write a new name for a family member that they have learned from their classmates.

Plenary

Activity: Review learning so far in the project with the following questions:

- *What topic have we been discussing?*
- *What did we find out about the families of Sofia, Arun and Marcus?*

Ask four or five learners to show their family drawing (or photo) to the class and to use it to talk about their family members. Ask other learners to listen and identify how the family described is similar or different from their own.

Ask four or five different learners to share the name of a family member and what they call them. Tell others in the class to put up their hand if they use the same word. Ask learners if they can see a pattern in the responses – for example, eight learners call their grandmother *Grandma*, and another five call her *Nanna*.

Answers and formative assessment: Open. Look for responses that show that learners can identify and share information about their family and its members.

Reflection: Refer learners to the learning goals in their books (I can say who is in my family, and I can find out if we all use the same names). See page xxiv for a suggested procedure.

Home learning ideas

Activity: Talk to a family member. Find out information about three more family members (e.g. their given names, what they are called and where they live).

Home–school link: Explain to parents/care givers that the learners will be working on a project on 'Families' in the coming weeks. Share with parents that the learners will be exploring the topic from different aspects – such as finding information from older family members, interviewing older family members, exploring the lives of family members. Share with parents/care givers that you seek their support in helping learners in gathering information, answering their questions and by encouraging them to talk about what they are doing in class about the project.

1.2 What have my family members taught me to do?

LEARNING OBJECTIVES: COMMUNICATION

1Cm.01 Communicating information: Answer questions with relevant information about a given issue

ADDITIONAL LEARNING OBJECTIVES

1Rs.04 Recording findings: Record information on a given issue in pictograms or simple graphic organisers

LEARNING GOALS

- I can talk about what I have learned from family members
- I can record answers in a chart

LEARNING ATTRIBUTES

This lesson gives learners the opportunity to be:

- Responsible for themselves, responsive to and respectful of others

Resources needed

Learner's Skills Book pages 16–20

Video 1

Downloadable 1.2 (table for use in 'How can I fill in a chart?')

Downloadable 1.3 (outline of 'Thank you' for use in 'How can I show I am grateful?')

Starter

Good for: Initiating learners to the idea that as we grow up, we learn things from people around us

Activity: Act out a few action words for the learners, such as driving a car, cooking, cleaning or writing. Ask learners to guess what you are doing, and write the word on the board. Ask: *Can a baby do these things? Do you think the baby will learn these things in time? How do you think we learn things as we grow up?*

What can we learn from our family members?

Good for: Learners to begin recognising that family members play a role in helping them learn many things

Activity:

1 Play the children the video for Project 1. Use the pictures from the video as prompts for class discussion. Show the picture of the learner riding a bicycle. Ask questions to initiate a discussion. *What is the child doing? How did he learn to ride a bike? Who do you think helped him to learn to ride the bike?*

Put learners in pairs to talk about the other two photos in the same way. *What is (he/she) learning how to do? Who is teaching (him/her) to do it?*

Ask whether the learners can do each of the things in the photos (riding a bike, tying their shoe laces, making a cake). *How did they learn? Did someone in the family show them how to do it? Who?* Take some examples from the class.

Share a personal example (real or made-up). For example, *My aunt taught me how to type. (When I was in college, I got a laptop but I didn't know how to type; my aunt used to work in an office so she knew how to type, and she taught me how to do it).*

Play a guessing game. Ask learners to guess who they think taught you a few things (again, real or made-up examples). For example, *Who do you think taught me to ride a bicycle? Who do you think taught me to read and write?*

2 Ask learners to think of some different things that they can do that someone showed them. Elicit some examples from the class. Prompt them, if necessary, with ideas appropriate to your learners (e.g. simple routine jobs such as laying the table, or more specific skills like playing a musical instrument, playing a sport, preparing something to eat, and so on). What things have learners learned to do on their own? What things have family members taught them? Encourage maximum sharing of ideas to ensure that all learners have been able to identify older members in the family who have taught them something.

Answers and formative assessment: *What are the learners doing in the pictures?* Picture 1: cycling, Picture 2: tying shoe laces, Picture 3: cooking, baking a cake and so on.

Who are they learning from? Possible answers for Pictures 1 and 2 is parent and picture 3 is grandparent. (The photos are open to some interpretation from the learners – accept any answer they can justify).

Differentiation:

Give support by playing the video several times through. Focus the learners on one question each time. Pause the video at relevant points and repeat the question. Suggesting a few activities for learners to choose from to help them identify different things that they have learned – packing my bag, putting toys away and so on.

Give extra challenge by dividing learners into small groups of three or four, and asking them to identify one thing that is common or the same that all have learned from an older family member. One learner from each group can share their response with the rest of the class. Put the response on the board or chart and ask learners to identify what is the most common things that most learners have learned from an older member of the family. If learners are unable to do so, prompt them to look at the information on the chart.

How can I fill in a chart?

Good for: Learners to learn how to record information in a simple tabular format based on personal information.

Activity:

1 Explain to learners that now it is time for them to make their own record of what they have learned from older family members.

Draw learners' attention to Zara's chart. Ask them to look at it and talk about what they can see. Point out the headings, and what is below each heading. Check understanding by asking learners what Zara can do and who has taught her each different thing. (Who do they think Mrs Ghulam might be? Perhaps a neighbour or a babysitter?)

Hand out downloadable 1.2 for the learners to fill the chart in by themselves. Display the completed chart. Demonstrate how to fill it in by asking a learner to come and put a tick against one of the illustrated activities that he/she can do, and then write who taught them how to do it (with support). Fill in the other illustrated rows of the chart in the same way.

For the blank rows, either ask the learners for suggestions of other activities you could include, or else fill in these rows with your own ideas appropriate to your learners. Invite volunteers from the class to fill in these new rows as above.

2 Now ask learners to fill in the chart independently (in the book or on the downloadable). Supervise learners while they are doing this. Encourage them to draw the activity they have learned how to do in the first column.

3 Read Marcus's speech bubble together, and ask a few volunteers to share their own examples from the chart using Marcus's example as a model (I have learned how to … My … taught me.'). Ask learners if anyone else can fly a kite, and whether their grandfather taught them. Is their answer the same as Marcus's or different to Marcus's? Tell learners to share their responses to the chart with their partners. Summarise by asking learners to name things (that they learned from older family members) that were the same as their partner and those that were different.

4 Ask learners if they could teach something to someone who is younger than them. Who would it be and what could they teach them? Record their answer.

Answers and formative assessment: Check whether learners are able to fill in the table themselves, in the same way that the process was modelled for them. Can they formulate questions to ask each other? Can they think of something appropriate to draw (or write) in the extra rows?

Differentiation:

Give support by helping learners with spellings. Give opportunities to selected learners to come up to the front of the class to fill in the chart so that you can check on, or reinforce their learning.

Give extra challenge by asking learners to work in pairs to think of three more things that they have learned from older family members. Get learners to dictate these things for their partner to write down. They could do this on a blank version of the chart. Put a large version of the chart on the board and ask pairs to share their responses.

How can I show that I am grateful?

Good for: Creating awareness and sensitivity among learners and giving them the opportunity to learn how to appropriately acknowledge when people help them.

Activity:

1 Explore the questions: *How do you feel when you have learned to do something by yourself? How do you share/express your feelings when you are happy that someone has helped you learn something?* Record the learners' responses on the board. Share with learners that Marcus was also happy and wanted to say thank you to his grandfather. (Check learners' understanding of grateful). Look at Marcus's ideas for how to do this.

Ask the learners to show what they think of each idea by drawing a smiley or sad face, and feed back as a class by having learners put up their hands to vote for each option.

2 Ask learners if they have any other ideas about how to show they are grateful. Encourage them to write or draw their ideas.

You can give out downloadable 1.3 for learners to colour the word THANK YOU. Encourage learners to use different colours and to add their own words or drawings which show what older family members do that they are grateful for. Create a display of the learners' artwork. (Set aside a few drawings for the final display at the end of the project).

Answers and formative assessment: Use the varied responses of the learners to develop perspective about how each learner has learned different things and how each learner has the opportunity to learn from different family members. Also, use learners' responses to assess their ability to identify what they have learned from older members of the family.

After learners have shared their responses to Marcus's suggestions, explore the issue further in the class: why do they think Marcus's ideas are good or not? Prompt learners to consider if the options are practical, possible for a learner to do, and so on.

Differentiation:

Give support by allowing thinking time and having learners work in pairs or small groups when they are judging the ideas that Marcus had. Allow them to discuss with each other before sharing their answers with the class.

Give extra challenge by expanding the discussion about teaching somebody younger by inviting learners to think of something they could teach their partner. Give the learners about 10 minutes to either teach or talk about a thing that they could teach their partner.

Plenary

Activity: Recap the learning from the lesson.

Put learners into groups of three. Display a chart similar to the one used during the lesson (make sure it is blank, but with the same headings). Ask one learner in each group: *Tell me one thing you have learned from a family member. Tell me who taught you how to do it.* Ask a second learner in each group to put that information on the chart. Ask the third learner to read out what is written on the chart. If you have a large class, you could put up two charts and divide the class into two for this.

Answers and formative assessment: Open. Having already carried out this task during the lesson, are learners now able to carry out the task independently?

Reflection: Refer learners to the learning goals in their books (I can talk about what I have learned from family members and I can fill in a chart). See page xxiv for a suggested procedure.

1.3 What can I find out in an interview?

LEARNING OBJECTIVES: RESEARCH

1Rs.01 Constructing research questions: Ask basic questions about a given issue

1Rs.02 Information skills: Talk about information on a given issue in sources provided

1Rs.03 Conducting research: Begin to participate in simple investigations and ask basic questions to find information and opinions

ADDITIONAL LEARNING OBJECTIVES

1E.01 Evaluating sources: Select a source relevant to a given issue and explain reasons for choice

LEARNING GOALS

- I can ask questions to find out about people's lives

LEARNING ATTRIBUTES

- Confident in working with information and ideas – their own and those of others

Resources needed

Learner's Skills Book pages 20–24

Audio 1 with transcript of Sofia interviewing her grandfather

A person for the interview – either a grandparent or an older staff member

Starter

Good for: Learners to practise listening and responding to simple questions. Also for learners to come up with simple questions that they can ask to get information out of the person they are interviewing.

Activity: Tell learners they are going to play a quick game in which they will be asking questions to gather information about the other people in the group. Invite two learners to the front of the class. Ask questions such as: *What is your favourite toy/game? How do you get to school? What is the first thing you do when you wake up in the morning?* Both learners can respond to the same questions, or each can be asked a different question.

Then put the whole class/group in threes and ask them to ask each other questions in the same way. With your guidance, ask one group of learners to demonstrate the activity for the whole class. Vary the game to suit your learners.

What questions can we ask in an interview?

Good for: Learners to understand that an interview is a good source to collect information from people.

Activity:

1 Explore with learners how they can get information – for example, *about a school, a place or a person*. Record their responses on the board. If one of the learners mentions getting information by asking somebody, then ask learners if they know what the word 'interview' means.

Tell learners that they are going to interview an older person and learn how to conduct an interview.

To learn more about interviews, they are going to listen to Sofia talking to her grandfather. Tell learners to listen carefully and pay attention to the questions that Sofia is asking her grandfather. Play the audio.
Ask learners to share the questions that they heard. Check answers.

2 Read the questions in the Learner's Skills Book with the learners. Play the audio again and ask them to talk about the answers to the questions with their partner.

Suggested answers:

1 Questions from the interview:

- Did you live in a town or in the countryside?
- How did you travel?
- What did you like doing with your family?
- What did you do in the evenings?
- How did your family keep in touch with people?
- How did you help your family?
- What did you learn from your parents or other older people around?

2 a Things he did: travelled by bus, played with his brother outside, played with trains, listened to the radio.

b People who taught him: his mother, his neighbour (Mrs Selma), his father, his teacher at school.

c Learners' own answers.

Differentiation:

Give support by before playing the audio, telling the learners some of the things they will hear about in the interview. Play a small section of the audio and ask them to identify Sofia's voice and the question she asked. Similarly, ask them to identify the grandfather's voice and how he responds to the question. Pause the audio at regular intervals to help learners to recall the question and the response.

Give extra challenge by asking learners to identify interviews they have seen on TV or heard on the radio, and to tell the class who was being interviewed and what information they gave. You could create a chart with pictures of the people interviewed and write a word to indicate what they were interviewed about – for example, Lionel Messi: football. Choose a few more personalities that would be relevant in your setting.

How do we interview a visitor?

Good for: Learners to review which kind of questions will generate the information they are looking for. Also good for helping learners to practise the skill of asking questions.

Activity:

Note: *For this activity, you will need to identify someone suitable who the learners can interview to get information about the person's childhood (e.g. a grandparent, or an older staff member). If the class is large, you may need to invite more than one person so the learners can conduct their interviews in small groups of six to eight.*

1 Remind learners that they will be interviewing somebody in class, so they need to prepare and plan for it. Talk about the visitor, and get the learners to write their name in the Learner's Skills Book.

2 Divide learners into small groups of three or four. Ask them to think of questions that they could ask to gather information about the person's childhood. Tell learners to look at the list for ideas about what to ask. After learners have made up some questions, ask each group to share their questions with other groups. Record the questions on the board/chart.

If a question is repeated, put a tick against the question to indicate this. Make sure that you keep the list of class questions for the next section.

3 Display the list of questions that the learners came up with.

Ask learners to choose five or six questions to use in the interview. When considering each question, ask learners to think about what information they would get if they asked that question.

Learners then copy their group's chosen questions into their book.

4 Ask learners to decide in their group who will ask each question, and to write their name next to the questions.

5 Talk about the importance of how you ask questions during an interview. Give a demonstration to learners of asking questions in two different ways: very softly and unclearly or louder and clearly, maintaining or not maintaining eye contact, and so on. In each case, ask the learners which is a better way of asking questions and why. Elicit from learners some good advice about how to ask questions in an interview – for example, *look at the person you are talking to, speak clearly, show interest and so on.*

Give learners 5 minutes to practise reading out their questions to each other. Monitor and give feedback.

6 Draw attention to the Useful Words given in this section, and also demonstrate how to acknowledge a response by smiling.

If you wish, you could also involve the learners in planning:

- how to prepare the room for the interview
- how to record the responses – either use a recording device or ask another teacher to note down the responses
- how to welcome the guest
- how to thank the guest for coming to school for the interview.

Carry out the interview.

Answers and formative assessment: Open.

Can learners identify which questions will get them the kind of information they are looking for? Can they adapt the questions or come up with alternatives if necessary? Can they explain why they have chosen (or not chosen) certain questions?

Differentiation:

Give support by helping learners both with formulating grammatically accurate questions and with selecting questions that will help get information. Also group learners carefully when they are preparing the questions so that they can support each other in putting questions together. Demonstrate the skills required to *ask* questions (orally), and giving each learner the opportunity to practise with the teacher. Prepare cue cards for the learners to ask their questions.

Give extra challenge by encouraging learners to ask follow-up questions (you could draw attention to the example from Sofia's interview where her grandfather talks about going to school in the town, so she follows this up by asking him how he travelled there). Demonstrate how to do this by sharing pieces of information about yourself and having learners think of follow-up questions to find out more (e.g. *When I'm on holiday, I like to go and see places* → *What kind of places do you like to see?*)

What did we learn from the interview?

1 Review with learners orally what they did in the interview. Ask learners: *Who did we interview? What did we find out?* Use the tick list in the book as a memory jogger, or provide a modified version if your interview covered very different topics from these. If learners worked in smaller groups to conduct the interview, ensure that they are with the same learners during this review.

2 Allow learners time to answer the questions independently. Then use questions such as the following to have a discussion that will help the learners reflect on the process of preparing and conducting the interview.

Why did you like about doing the interview?
Why did you not like about doing the interview?
What did you find out that was interesting?
Did you find it easy or difficult to do the interview? Why? What things should we do differently when we do an interview again?

3 Tell learners that you want them to do a similar interview with someone they know (someone in their family or someone who looks after them). Ask them to think about who they would like to interview and write their name in their book.

Answers and formative assessment: Listen carefully to the learners' responses to questions asked them to review the interview process. (Ensure that as many learners as possible have an opportunity to respond to at least one question).

Are they able to evaluate what they learned: What was interesting? What went well/not so well? What could they do differently?

Differentiation:

Give support by grouping learners so that they can support each other both during the interview and the review process. Offer opportunities to practise asking the questions they plan to use for their family member interview.

Give extra challenge by asking learners to include extra questions in their family member interview (i.e. in addition to the ones they used for the class visitor) so that they can get more information.

Plenary

Activity: Display the following statements about the interview with the visitor (or adapt them to match what you did):

1 We asked __________ [name of the visitor] questions
2 We prepared five questions.
3 We recorded the answers by __________ [e.g. videoing the interview, taking notes, using an audio recorder].
4 We practised asking the question clearly.

Tell learners that you have written what they did but in the wrong order. Ask them to put the four statements in the correct order. Ask: *What can we find out when we interview somebody? Is it a good way to find out information? Why/why not?*

Answers: Correct sequence = 2, 4, 1, 3.

Reflection: Refer Learners to the learning goals in their books (I can ask questions to find out about my family members' lives). See page xxiv for a suggested procedure.

Home learning ideas

Activity: Learners interview a family member (or other appropriate adult) at home. Ask learners to share orally who they will interview. Ask them to think about: What five questions will they ask? Whose help will they ask for at home to record the interview?

Home–school link: If the school has a digital space that is shared with parents or for parents to share or access, ask them to send snippets of the interview if it was recorded. Alternatively, they could send a note in detailing their observation about the learner conducting the interview at home. If appropriate, collate the information gathered from the parents and create a page or link to share it.

1.4 What else can I find out from my family members?

LEARNING OBJECTIVES: REFLECTION

1Rf.03 Personal perspectives: Talk about what has been learned during an activity, with support

LEARNING GOALS

- I can learn stories, games and interesting facts from older people

LEARNING ATTRIBUTES

This lesson gives learners the opportunity to be:

- Engaged intellectually and socially, ready to make a difference

Note: *This lesson provides examples for learners of what they might be able to learn from the adults who are close to them. They learn about a festival celebrated by the family (from looking at an old photo), an old family story and a simple game. It is intended that learners then find out about and share similar information, stories or games from their own families/care givers, so you will need to communicate with the relevant adults to arrange this. (See Home Learning ideas below). Depending on how* *you are organising your time spent on this project, you may ask learners and their families to choose what they would like to share after the whole lesson; alternatively, you could work on the lesson section by section, asking families to share information about a festival, a story or a game after each section.*

Resources needed

Learner's Skills Book pages 24–28

Audio 2 with transcript of Arun talking about his grandmother

Starter

Good for: Learners to explore interactions with family members at social events, what happens at social events, who they meet or similar.

Activity: Introduce this session by asking these questions:

- *Who can tell me about a party they have had with their family?*
- *Why did your family have a party?*
- *Who came for the party?*
- *What did you do?*
- *What did you like?*

Take all the responses from the learners. Tell learners that they are going to spend some time finding out about a special kind of party that Arun learned about from his grandmother. Tell them the party is for a festival: has anyone been to a festival? Do they know what it is?

What can we find out about a festival?

Good for: Learners to explore how festivals are celebrated, what family members do during festivals and also the significance of family celebrations.

Activity:

1 Read the text in the book together. Explain that Arun, Zara and Sofia are going to share what they found out from the older people who they know. Then later, learners will be able to find out about stories, games and festivals from their own family.

Draw attention to the photo of Arun's grandmother celebrating Diwali. Why do the learners think it is a black-and-white photograph?

Read through the first set of questions with the learners. Tell them to listen out for the answers as they listen. Play the audio. Check the answers.

2 Repeat the audio. Learners answer the two further questions with their partner.

Ask learners if they think one of their relatives might be able to share information about a family celebration. Who could they ask?

Suggested answers:

1 a Diwali (also called the Festival of Lights).

b Answers may include some of the following: Naani's family decorated the house, they made sweets and snacks, they wore new clothes, they visited their friends and family, they burned firecrackers.

2 Open.

Differentiation:

Give support by talking about the photo (and about Diwali) before the audio is shared, drawing attention to details such as the lamps, flowers and so on so that learners can make the connection when they listen to the audio.

Give extra challenge by asking learners to name other festivals where families get together for a meal or visit each other, where they decorate their homes, where they set off firecrackers, or similar. Use local festivals when discussing: give clues and elicit responses.

What stories can we find out?

Good for: Learners to learn about the lives of their family members from stories, and to think about why old family stories are important

Activity:

1 Draw learners' attention to the picture of the bell. Tell them that the bell is important in the story: can they guess why? Read the story aloud. Check understanding of words such as thorn and bandage.

2 Ask learners to write their responses. Review the responses from learners orally.

3 Ask learners to share the questions with their partner. Invite a few learners to share their answers with the class, then extend the discussion by asking whether anyone in their family has shared stories about their childhood. Can they remember any story in particular? What do stories like that tell

us about the life of the people then? What can we learn from these stories about people's lifestyles, relationships or similar before we were born?

Suggested answers:

2 a Zara's aunt told her the story. **b** The doctor took out a thorn, bandaged the old man's leg and gave him a walking stick. **c** People rang the bell to say thank you to the doctor. **d** Learners may suggest yes, because Zara's aunt heard the bell ring 'many times' (therefore a lot of patients must have wanted to thank the doctor).

Differentiation:

Give support by using flash cards to introduce or highlight the new words in the story prior to reading the text. Ask learners to read in pairs so that they can support each other.

Give extra challenge by asking learners to retell the story in a group.

What games can we find out about?

Good for: Learners to find out about games they can learn from older people, and to compare them with the kind of games they play now.

Activity:

1 Draw attention to the picture of the completed game of 'Dots and Boxes' that Sofia's neighbour Maria taught her. Read the instructions with the learners. Can the learners work out who won the game between Sofia and Maria? (Sofia – there are more 'S's than 'M's).

2 Get learners to share their responses to the questions with their partner, then feed back as a class. Talk about the kind of games that learners play now: What kind of games do they play? Who taught them to play? If the games are played on phones, tablets or other, explore why Sofia's neighbour Maria might not have played games like that.

Suggested answers and formative assessment:

1 Learners' own answers.

2 Are learners able to talk about the kind of games they play? Are they able to make comparisons with those games and the game in the activity? Are they able to think of reasons why other people might play (or have played) different games?

Differentiation:

Give support by reading each instruction and allowing the learners to play the game one step at a time.

Give extra challenge by inviting learners to find similar games that can be played with classmates and teach others to play them.

Plenary

Activity: Ask learners *why* they think older people may have a lot of interesting things to share. Prompt them by asking them to think of an older person that they know: do they know where that person lived when they were a child, what job(s) they did when they were younger, whether they have travelled? Discuss that they probably have interesting things to say about their experiences. They might be able to share information with them about a festival they celebrated, an interesting family story or a game they used to play as a child. You could also discuss when learners think might be a good time to talk to 'their' older person.

Answers: Learners' own answers

Reflection: Refer learners to the learning goals in their books (I can learn stories, games and interesting facts from older people). See page xxiv for a suggested procedure.

Home learning ideas

Activity: Ask learners to gather information from older family members or people who help look after them. They could find out about a festival and its celebration, a game or a story. Over a week get each learner to share what they have gathered during snack or break time. Ensure that all learners have the opportunity to share

Home–school link: Update parents on what learners have been doing in the project (exploring how older people spent their childhood). Ask parents/care givers or other family members to share their experiences, show photographs, pictures or things around the house that can help learners get an idea about what their lives have been like.

1.5 How can we show what we have learned?

LEARNING OBJECTIVES: COMMUNICATION

1Cm.01 Communicating information: Answer questions with relevant information about a given issue

1Cm.02 Listening and responding: Listen to others in class discussions and respond with simple questions

ADDITIONAL LEARNING OBJECTIVES

1A.04 Solving problems: Choose a possible solution to an issue from a range of actions given

LEARNING GOALS

- I can show other people what I have learned from my family

LEARNING ATTRIBUTES

This lesson gives learners the opportunity to be:

- Confident in working with information and ideas – their own and those of others

Resources needed

Learner's Skills Book pages 28–31

Downloadable 1.4 (template for display)

Starter

Good for: Helping learners to recall what they have done in past sessions in order to prepare the display that they will create in this unit.

Activity: Play a game where you say a word/phrase and learners have to say a word that is associated to it based on what was done in past sessions. Suggested words/phrases: *family members, names, interview, stories, festivals, games, learn from family members.*

How can we make a display about the people who taught us things?

Good for: Learners to explore different ways of sharing information that they have collected.

Activity: Ask learners to suggest ways of sharing the information they have gathered during the project. How can they tell others about the older people that have helped them? Record the responses on the board. Tell learners that they are going to learn about creating a display.

If possible, take the learners on a walk around the school premises to look at different kinds of displays. Ask them to observe them carefully – look at what is drawn, what is written, what the colours used are. Do they have borders? Where are the displays located? Back in class, discuss what the learners found out about displays.

Draw attention to what Marcus has made for his display. Ask learners to identify what information Marcus has shared in the picture and writing.

1. Recap for the learners about the different things they have learned from older people. Ask them to think about and write down the name of one person that has taught them something and to tick one of the options showing what that person taught them (or write it as 'Something else').
2. Give each learner a blank sheet of paper or a copy of downloadable 1.4. Ask learners to draw a picture of the person – write that person's name and write what they have taught them. Invite them to colour and decorate their picture.

   Gather the learners' individual portraits and summaries together and make a large display. Add a suitable title.

Answers and formative assessment: Open. Please note that the learners' skill or ability to draw should not be prioritised for this task.

Differentiation:

Give support by helping learners to spell words in the text that they would like to include. Help them locate information from previous pages if required.

Give extra challenge by asking learners to include something in their illustration that represents what their family member has taught them (e.g. if it was something about a festival, they could draw an object representing the festival).

How will we tell people more about what we learned?

Good for: Learners to find ways to extend or share more information.

Activity:

1 Remind learners about what Marcus did for his class display. Marcus has told his classmates about what he learned from his grandmother: she told him a story about looking after a baby bird. *What are the different ways that Marcus can share more information about the baby bird story?* List learners' responses on the board. Prompt them, if necessary, to suggest ways that he could do this, which might include telling the story about the bird (orally), writing it down, drawing a picture, acting it out and so on.

2 Tell learners that now it is their turn to share more information about what they learned from the older person they drew for their display. They need to think of the best way to do this. Ask them to mark their choice by circling one or more options from the list supplied. Tell them to talk about their ideas with a partner (or with you). Group learners according to their chosen option(s). If the group consists of learners who have chosen to act out what they learned, ask: *How will you show the actions for…? Will you need any special things?* Support learners with choosing an effective way to share the information they have learned from 'their' older person. Allow time for them to prepare for this and to practise if necessary. Remind them to think about any props they might need (e.g. if they are going to demonstrate a game that they have learned). Plan time for each learner to present what they are sharing to the class (or to their group). You may wish to take photos of learners if they are demonstrating a game or performing a mime – for example, so that you can include this on the display wall.

Formative assessment: Are learners able to come up with ideas for conveying what they have found out through pictures, acting, writing or similar?

Differentiation:

Give support by explaining the options given and talking to the learner about what each option might involve.

Give extra challenge by asking learners to think of another possible way to share what they have learned. Ask them to explain which way might be better, and why.

How can we answer questions from our classmates?

Good for: Learners to consider what they can learn from and share with their classmates by asking and answering questions.

Activity: Ask all the learners to look at the display wall and, if possible, to see how other groups have shared their information through drawing, mime, writing or similar.

Tell the learners that we can find out more information by asking questions. What questions can we ask about what other learners have displayed? Encourage learners to think of one good question to ask, based on the particular display(s) they are looking at. Encourage the learners who created the display to give an answer. Talk about how learners could reply if they *do not* know the answer to the question: they could have a sensible guess (*I think probably …*) or they could say that they will try to find out. Emphasise that this is fine!

What does the display tell us? How can we appreciate what other learners have shared?

If possible, invite learners and teachers from other classes and have the learners talk to them about their display.

Answers: Open, based on learner participation and experience.

Differentiation:

Give support by giving an example of how to ask a question about the display and then prompting learners with a question word that they could use to create their own question.

Give extra challenge by encouraging learners to ask focused follow-up questions in discussion by asking them questions such as *Is there anything more you would like to know about what (name) said?*

Plenary

Activity: Gather learners around the display, ask each learner to choose a display of another classmate and say what the illustration shows. Draw learners' attention to a range of different things that learners have learned from older members in the family.

Answers: Open, based on what each learner can see and talk about from the illustrations in the display.

Reflection: Refer learners to the learning goals in their books (I can show other people what I have learned from my family). See page xxiv for a suggested procedure.

Home learning ideas

Home–school link: Send an image home of the display created with all the illustrations made by the learners. If there is an opportunity for parents/care givers to come to school, ask them to write feedback about the display on sticky notes and add these to the display.

1.6 What did we enjoy doing?

LEARNING OBJECTIVES: REFLECTION

1Rf.03 Personal perspectives: Talk about what has been learned during an activity with support

1Rf.04 Personal learning: Talk about something liked in a particular activity

LEARNING GOALS

- I can talk about something I liked

LEARNING ATTRIBUTES

This lesson gives learners the opportunity to be:

- Reflective as learners, developing their ability to learn

Resources needed

Learner's Skills Book pages 31–33

Downloadable 1.5 (enlarged version of 'New things I have found out')

Starter

Good for: Encouraging learners to begin to recall and share examples of learning from the project.

Activity: Provide a box or bag of counters in two colours (e.g. red and blue). Tell learners to pick up a counter without looking. If it is red, the learner has to say something they found out from their own family, and if it is blue, they have to say something about one of their classmates' families. (The latter should be based on something in their classmates' display or something their classmate has talked about).

What have I found out about families?

Good for: Learners to review the whole project and identify what they have learned.

Activity: Recap the whole project in sequence, displaying pages from the Learner's Skills Book. You can also point out other drawings, charts or images of learner responses to questions, as appropriate.

Hand out downloadable 1.5 for the learners to fill in. Draw learners' attention to the four boxes. Ask a few learners to share with the class what they would like to write or draw in each box.

Ask learners to fill out these pages independently.

Answers and formative assessment: Look for appropriate responses that demonstrate understanding of the topics covered during the project.

Differentiation:

Give support by asking learners what they would specifically write or draw in each box. Ask them to verbalise before they start. Use questions if required to prompt learners to remember.

Give extra challenge by asking learners to share with the class how they have filled in their table, explaining what they have written/drawn and why.

How did I feel about it?

Good for: Learners to explore their feelings about various activities while working on this project.

Activity: Remind learners about the various activities the class carried out during the project. Each time you mention an activity, ask learners to indicate how they felt about it (choose a suitable method appropriate to your setting – for example, drawing a face on a whiteboard, thumbs up or down, hands up or hands on their head, and so on).

Ask learners to fill in the given chart, independently, after first checking that they understand what to do.

Differentiation:

Give support by asking learners to share their responses verbally first and checking which symbol they would draw. Assist learners in reading the text in the first column.

Give extra challenge by asking learners to share the reason for their assessment, and also exploring (if they did not much like the activity) what aspect of the activity they would like to change next time.

Have I learned how to do something new?

Good for: Helping learners to reflect on things that they have done for the first time and identify a new skill that they have learned.

Activity: Ask learners to go through the pages of this project in the Learners' Skills Book carefully and write the letter 'N' (new) on the page if it had an activity or some information that was 'new' for the learners.

Ask the learners to select any one thing that was new for them and write it on page 33.

Differentiation:

Give support by asking learners to talk about their responses first and then assist them in framing the sentence if required.

Give extra challenge by asking learners to share what about the activity was new. Would they like to do the activity again? How do they feel when they are doing something for the first time?

Plenary

Activity: Share with the learners the best parts of the project from your point of view, such as your observations about how well the learners shared, contributed and so on. Give examples of interesting answers given by learners, positive feedback from parents and other teachers, and anywhere else that may be relevant.

Reflection: Refer learners to the learning goals in their books (I can talk about what I liked). See page xxiv for a suggested procedure.

Home learning Ideas

Activity: Recap all home learning ideas that were done through the project with the learners in class. Ask learners to say which home learning ideas they liked and why. Learners can share the responses in class before they begin the next project.

Home–school link: Combine all the home–school links into a single document and share with the parents that the project on families has been concluded. Tell them about any highlights and interesting learner responses that emerged during the project. Thank parents for all their support.

Taking it further

This project will have helped learners to explore the different kinds of families that there are and the role that families play in their growing up years. The project also has the potential to build closer and fruitful ties between the school and the families of the learners.

Celebration of days like Grandparents' Day or a day to invite family members or care givers can be organised if the school policy allows for it. It would be a positive way to acknowledge and thank families for the role they play in the lives of learners and for the support they extend to the school.

Learners who have successfully completed this project will have developed a range of skills and attributes that would enable them to attempt the Cambridge International Primary Global Perspectives Challenges 'Growing and growing up' and 'Learning new things' with enhanced confidence.

2 What kind of garden would be best?

Introduction

To begin with, learners look at an image that shows the characters engaged in various activities in a community garden. You will want to allow the discussion to build on elements of the learners' own experiences. Give time for learners to think about their own responses before opening up discussions in pairs or groups.

Learners ask and answer questions about gardens (Lesson 1 Analysis). They consider their prior understanding of the nature and purpose of gardens based on their own experience. They consider different people's perspectives as well as their own.

Then learners find out about what other learners in the class would like to have in a garden (Lesson 2 Research) in a simple investigation. As part of their research, they devise questions. The learners find out what other members of their group think, and they present their findings using pictograms.

The learners develop their understanding of appropriate sources of information by asking whether a given source is useful or not for their enquiry (Lesson 3 Evaluation). They identify sources that will help them understand what plants are good to grow in a garden, what things other than plants are useful in a garden and what jobs need to be done.

The learners next use the knowledge and understanding gained of different people's perspectives on gardens to create a model (Lesson 4 Collaboration). They use this model as part of imaginative play to explore how different groups of people would feel about their proposed design.

Then they use the models that they have created to tell other learners about their ideas (Lesson 5 Communication) and they ask questions about other learners' models. Following their study of other learners' designs, they explain which ideas they think are most appealing to them personally. They are also challenged to explain which of the ideas they have seen are most appropriate for their school and why.

Finally, they reflect (Lesson 6 Reflection) on what they have learned about gardens. They are also asked to consider what new knowledge, skills and understanding they have developed, with support. Additionally, they consider what aspects of the project they have enjoyed.

Cross-curricular links and themes

This project lends itself particularly well to integration with theme-based learning on plants, animals and nature in the world around us.

The theme of sustainable food production developed throughout this project builds understanding relevant to the UN Sustainable Development Goal 2: End hunger, achieve food security and improved nutrition and promote sustainable agriculture, and UN Sustainable Development Goal 15: Protect, restore and promote sustainable use of terrestrial ecosystems, sustainably manage forests, combat desertification, halt and reverse land degradation and halt biodiversity loss.

The theme of learners' participation in sustainable food production builds understanding of their right to good food. This fits with the UN Convention on the Rights of the Child Article 24: Every child has the right to the best possible health. Governments must provide good quality health care, clean water, nutritious food, a clean environment and education on health and wellbeing so that children can stay healthy. Richer countries must help poorer countries achieve this.

The learners' design ideas for the school environment builds understanding of Article 12: Every child has the right to give their opinions freely on issues that affect them. Adults should listen and take learners seriously.

Learners have opportunities to apply their knowledge and understanding of, and skills in:	
Scientific skills	• Exploring ways that different animals and plants inhabit local environments • Considering what plants need to grow • Considering how food grown in gardens can contribute to a healthy diet
Mathematical skills	• Answering a question by sorting and organising data using pictograms and discussing the results
Speaking and listening skills	• Speaking clearly and choosing words carefully to express their ideas about gardens • Answering questions about their design ideas and explaining them further when asked • Engaging in imaginative play, and enacting how different people would react to their garden ideas
Reading skills	• Reading and listening to a range of garden-themed books, drawing on background information and vocabulary provided • Making links from their reading to their own experiences of gardens • Demonstrating their understanding of explicit meaning in texts, labels, lists and captions to find relevant information about gardens
Technological skills	• Using their hands and fingers with increasing confidence, coordination control and fluency by having the opportunity to accurately manipulate materials and tools while creating their model garden.

Before beginning work on this project, it would be helpful if learners have knowledge of or have had previous experience of:
• Speaking to a group to share an experience • Answering questions and explaining further when asked • Answering questions by sorting and organising data or objects in a variety of ways – for example, using block graphs and pictograms with practical resources; discussing the results • Understanding that texts for different purposes look different – for example, use of photographs, diagrams • Recognising different parts of a book – for example, title page, contents and understanding their functions • Creating designs and making models using simple tools and materials • Engaging in imaginative play, enacting simple characters or situations

Sustainability links and themes
The stewardship theme of caring for plants and animals in familiar local spaces throughout this project builds understanding relevant to the UN Sustainable Development Goal 15: Protect, restore and promote sustainable use of terrestrial ecosystems, and UN Sustainable Development Goal 2: End hunger, achieve food security and improved nutrition and promote sustainable agriculture. The theme of active participation in gardening builds understanding relevant to Article 24 of the UN Rights of the Child. This says that learners and young people have the right to be both physically and mentally fulfilled. This project builds understanding of gardening as a source of good nourishing food and as a means of constructing a safe and healthy environment.

Assessment focus
The focus skills for this project are Evaluation and Research. The following downloadables will support you with assessing learners' attainment against the curriculum framework:
• Downloadable 2.10 (Assessment guidance sheet: Evaluation)
• Downloadable 2.11 (Assessment record sheet: Evaluation)
• Downloadable 2.12 (Assessment guidance sheet: Research Part 1)
• Downloadable 2.13 (Assessment record sheet: Research Part 1)
For a general introduction to the Approach to Assessment in this course, see page xxiii

Getting started

Good for: Activating learners' prior understanding of gardens – their uses and different people's perspectives on activities that take place in them.

Activity:

1 Focus on the picture and ask the learners what kind of place this is (a garden).

Explain that you are going to start by repeating a chant about what the people are doing: read through the words of the chant together (providing support with vocabulary as necessary). Repeat the chant with Audio 3. Can learners point to the people in the picture doing the activities in red print?

2 Provide support with the vocabulary for things shown in the picture as necessary. Talk/ask about the picture using some of the following suggested questions.

- *Would this be a nice place to visit?* What makes the learners think so?
- Point to Marcus who is watering with a watering can. *Why is this an important job? What other jobs are important to do in a garden?*
- *What is this?* (Point to the apple tree). Do the learners like eating apples? Have they ever eaten an apple or another fruit from a tree? (Establish that it is important to ask an adult first before eating something you have picked to ensure that it is safe to do so). Have the learners seen fruit growing in a garden? What have they seen? Where was this?
- Point to the flowering plant. *What is flying near the flowers?* (A bee) Have they seen flowers growing in a garden? Where?
- Point to Sofia. *What is she doing? Why?* (She is helping to plant flowers). What flowers do the learners like? Have they seen flowers growing in a garden? Where?
- Point out the trowel. *What is this used for? What other tools do you need if you want to look after a garden?*
- Point out the small vegetable plot. *Are these flowers? What is growing here?* Do the learners recognise any of the vegetables? Have they tried any vegetables picked fresh from the garden? If they could choose which ones to grow, what might they like to try growing? Have they ever helped to grown any vegetables – or do they know anyone who grows vegetables? What jobs are needed to look after them?
- Point out the man and the woman. *What are they doing?*
- Point out the minibeast hotel. *What could this be used for?* Then ask about the bird feeder. What animals can they see in the garden? What animals have they seen in other gardens? Why is it important to look after animals and insects?
- Point out Arun. *Why might it be nice to sit in a garden and read a book?* Have the learners done this? Or do they know someone who does this?

Answers: This will depend on the learner's prior experience and their interests. It is useful for the rest of the project to draw out some of the following aspects of gardens:

- They have a variety of functions (e.g. decorative, functional, recreational).
- Different people enjoy gardens for different purposes at different times.
- Gardens can provide fresh, tasty vegetables and fruit.

- Gardens also provide food and shelter for a range of animals (birds, insects, etc)..
- Gardening can be hard work (it involves a lot of different jobs) but it is also very rewarding.
- Gardens are also a place for rest and recreation. People enjoy fresh air and being close to nature so they make gardens in whatever spaces that they have.

Differentiation:

Give support by providing images of gardens that the learners have direct experience of and asking them to describe activities that take place there prior to looking at the image in the book.

Give extra challenge by providing images of gardens taken in contrasting locations. *How are the gardens similar or different? Why might gardens look different in different places? What different kinds of activities might take place in different kinds of gardens? Do people do the same activities in gardens all year or do they change? Why?*

2.1 What is a garden?

LEARNING OBJECTIVES: ANALYSIS

1A.01 Identifying perspectives: Say something known about an issue

LEARNING GOALS

- I can say what I know about gardens

LEARNING ATTRIBUTES

This lesson gives learners the opportunity to be:

- Confident in working with information and ideas – their own and those of others

Resources needed

Learner's Skills Book pages 36–38

Downloadable 2.1 (picture frame and space for learners to write about a garden they know)

Downloadable 2.8 (model dialogue)

Audio 4 with transcript of Shazia, Afua and Romario talking about their gardens

Paper or a notebook for drawing a garden

If possible, photos of places local to your area (and which learners may be familiar with) where people grow plants

Starter

Good for: Formative assessment of the learners' understanding of the issue before any input. Learners who consistently point appropriately may well need further challenge. Learners who consistently point incorrectly may well need additional support.

Activity: Tell the learners that we will be finding out all about things that people like to do in gardens. Name an activity – for example, *planting flowers. Is this something that people like to do in their gardens?* Ask learners to: Point to the window if you think 'yes'. Point to the door if you think 'no'. Point to the ceiling if you think 'maybe'. Repeat with a range of activities relevant to your setting. Choose some that are almost certainly not garden activities (e.g. 'using a vacuum cleaner') and some that are (e.g. cutting grass, growing oranges, sitting having a drink, playing with a ball).

What can we do in a garden?

Good for: Learners to gain confidence in talking about the issue of gardens; their similarities and differences.

Activity: Ask learners to work with a partner. They should look at the three photos and discuss the four questions together. Take feedback as a class.

Answers and formative assessment: Listen to check whether learners answer the questions appropriately. Learners' answers will vary, but they may be objective (e.g. relating to the kind of plants in the photos), or subjective (e.g. the people are happy). Both are equally appropriate. Learners may pick up on the nature of the activities, relaxation, a game, growing vegetables and/or the plants they can see. They may talk about who is in each garden.

Differentiation:

Give support by sharing the dialogue in downloadable 2.8 in which the characters model this discussion. Can they spot things that they have missed?

Give extra challenge by asking learners about how the features of each garden are appropriate to their use – for example, *Why is the second garden a good place to play cricket?*

What different kinds of garden are there?

Good for: Building understanding that gardens come in different shapes and sizes and that people have different perspectives on their use.

Activity:

1. Focus attention on the photos of gardens. Ask what the learners can see in each garden, and ask how they are different from each other. Explain the matching task, demonstrating how to draw a line from the person to their garden. Then ask learners to listen to the three people talking about their gardens. Play Audio 4, pointing out when each character begins speaking. Repeat the recording if needed. Encourage the learners to complete the activity. Check answers.
2. Focus attention on sentences a–c and the words in the box. Explain the task. Listen again to the audio. Learners complete the cloze text (by placing the missing words into the provided sentences).
3. Focus on the photo of Marcus and read the speech bubble together. Ask learners to talk with their partner about which garden is best for Marcus, then take feedback as a class. Model how to write the correct garden number in the sentence.
4. Tell learners to work in pairs to discuss which garden is best for them.

Suggested answers:

1. Shazia: garden 2; Afua: garden 3; Romario: garden 1
2. **a** small; **b** vegetable; **c** butterfly
3. Garden 3. Can learners explain why they think that garden is best for Marcus?
4. Learners' own answers. Can learners explain why their chosen garden is best for them?

Differentiation:

Give support by modelling a process of elimination. Point to the veg box. *What is this? Does Shazia grow vegetables?* (No) *Does Romario?* (No) *So whose garden must this be?*

Give extra challenge by asking learners to complete the following sentences:

- Shazia likes …
- Afua likes …
- Romario goes to … because …

What kind of garden have you seen?

Good for: Learners to apply the understanding about gardens gained in the previous sections to their own context.

Activity:

1. Explain that we have now seen some different kinds of gardens. Recap: *What do people use them for? How are they similar? How are they different?* Ask learners to draw a garden that they have seen. If you wish, use downloadable 2.1 for this. Establish that this could be a park (a kind of public garden), and that gardens can be different shapes and sizes, and that even very small spaces (e.g. a balcony) can be used to grow things. Invite learners to draw someone in the garden, if they wish, doing something appropriate – discuss that people enjoy being in gardens for various reasons.
2. Model how to talk about a garden using the questions provided. Get learners to ask and answer the questions about their own pictures in pairs. (Space is provided in the downloadable so that learners can write down their answers to the questions in the Learner's Skills Book, if appropriate).

Answers and formative assessment: Open. Use the pictures learners have drawn, and their answers in Question 2, to check whether learners can convey something they know about gardens.

Differentiation:

Give support by providing some images of local gardens for learners to draw. Ask learners to read their work back to you, and describing writing that is unclear.

Give extra challenge by asking learners to write a caption on the downloadable about what the person is doing in the garden as well as why they are doing it.

Probe learners' answers. What does this person know (about jobs in the garden) or enjoy (about being in their garden)?

Plenary

Activity: Display some learners' responses to 'What kind of garden have you seen?' Ask the learners to describe the gardens they have drawn and (if appropriate) the activities taking place in them. *What plants are growing there? What would it feel like to be in that garden?* Display more than one. *How are these gardens similar? How are they different?* Draw out from discussions the idea that the form a garden takes depends on its use. This in turn reflects the needs and wants of the people that use it. The nature of the activities that can take place also depend on other factors, such as the weather and the space that is available.

Suggested answers: Open. Look for responses that comment on the gardens appropriately based on the learners's own experiences.

Reflection: Refer learners to the learning goals in their books (I can say what I know about gardens). See page xxiv for a suggested procedure.

Home learning ideas

Activity: Ask learners to keep their eyes open for gardens when they are out and about. Where do people grow plants? What different kinds of plants can they see around them? Alternatively, what kind of gardens do they see in the media, or in books?

Home–school link: Tell parents/care givers that the children are investigating gardens in class. Ask them to talk to the learners about their own garden or other gardens they visit or know, what they are like and how they use them. They could also take their children to visit a local park.

2.2 How can I find out what children in my class think about gardens?

LEARNING OBJECTIVES: RESEARCH

1Rs.01 Constructing research questions: Ask basic questions about a given issue

1Rs.03 Conducting research: Begin to participate in simple investigations and ask basic questions to find information and opinions

LEARNING GOALS

- I can make a chart that shows learners' ideas

LEARNING ATTRIBUTES

This lesson gives learners the opportunity to be:

- Responsible for themselves, responsive to and respectful of others

Resources needed

Learner's Skills Book pages 39–41

Downloadable 2.2 (a table for learners to use in their survey)

Downloadable 2.8 (model dialogue)

Audio recording 5 with transcript of Sofia talking to her friends.

Starter

Good for: Introducing learners to the idea of handling data for use in investigations about people's opinions.

Activity: Show learners three flowers (or three pictures). Number them 1–3. Ask learners to think about which one is their favourite. Display a simple blank chart like downloadable 2.2 with flower numbers 1–3 in each row (or a picture of each flower). Point to the flowers in turn. Take a vote by asking them to raise their hands if that flower is their favourite. Record the vote by drawing a smiley face for each vote. Get the learners to count with you as you draw. Ask questions to test understanding –

for example, *Which flower did most people like? How do we know that (from the chart)?*

Give extra challenge by moving learners quickly to the next section if they easily understand this data-gathering and recording process.

How can we use pictures to show our ideas?

Good for: Demonstrating the process of participating in simple investigations and asking basic questions to find information and opinions.

Activity:

1 Explain to the learners how the characters in the book are developing their ideas for a school garden. Explain the purpose of the symbols and chart shown in the book. Check understanding by asking learners to point to the picture representing each item in the chart (plants for the butterflies, fruit to pick and minibeast hotel).

2 Play Audio 5 (the characters conducting a survey about which idea they like best for a school garden). Ask learners to tell you Sofia's question. Ask learners how many learners want plants for the butterflies. Play the audio again and elicit the answer.

3 Check understanding of how Sofia has filled in the chart. (Why has she drawn three smiley faces next to the 'Plants for butterflies' picture?) Ask learners to add their own choice to the chart. Check understanding of 'popular' and get learners to write the answer to the question.

   When learners have finished questioning and filling in the chart, ask them to look at their chart and see what they have found out. Tell them to record their group's most popular idea in their book by drawing an appropriate symbol to represent the idea and by naming it in the spaces provided.

Answers and formative assessment:

2 Would you like plants for the butterflies, fruit to pick or a hotel for the bugs?

3 Plants for the butterflies is the most popular response. Learner's own favourite is open.

   Can learners show understanding of how the chart works by adding their own favourite?

Differentiation:

Give support by pausing the audio clip after each character has completed their line. Demonstrate how to record each character's choice on the chart – for example, *Where should I put the smiley face for Arun?*

What questions can we ask?

Good for: Forming a question that is suitable for a simple investigation to find opinions.

Activity:

1 Divide the learners into groups. Each group first discusses ideas for things that they would like to see in a school garden. Encourage a range of suggestions: learners do not have to copy the ideas that the characters suggested. If necessary, show the photos from 2.1 to prompt ideas. Model how to use the sentence frame provided to write their question.

2 Give each group a copy of downloadable 2.2. Support learners in completing the chart with pictures relevant to the three things that their group has chosen.

Answers and formative assessment: Open. Can learners make up a question using the three suggestions made in the group?

Differentiation:

Give support by displaying and reading the characters' dialogue (downloadable 2.8) with the learners before they start on their own discussion. Clarify that they are thinking of ideas for good things to have in a garden for their school. Check their understanding using the questions provided.

Suggest appropriate symbols for the learners' ideas. Provide a worked example using the learners' own suggestions and responses.

Give extra challenge by asking learners to record not only the number of learners who expressed a given preference, but also their reason for doing so. *[Name] wants a [idea] because …*

What did we find out?

Good for: Beginning to recognise ways in which data can show information about an issue.

Activity:

1 Learners conduct their own surveys using their chart. Remind them to use the question they agreed on (Would you like …?) and to record the answer in the chart by drawing a smiley face. Tell them how many learners they should ask the question

to, or how long they have to ask as many learners as possible.

2 When learners have finished questioning and filling in the chart, ask them to look at their chart and see what they have found out. Tell them to record their group's most popular idea in their book. Tell them to draw an appropriate symbol to represent the idea and name it in the spaces provided.

Answers and formative assessment: Open. Check that what learners say about their data accurately reflects what they have shown by asking questions such as *How many learners liked the x idea?* *Is this more or less than the number of learners who liked the y idea?*

Differentiation:

Give support by working through the process of how to ask the first question and recording on the chart with groups of learners who find this process challenging. Remind learners how Sofia asked questions and recorded responses with her group.

Give extra challenge by challenging them to draw some possible simple conclusions from their data. *More learners like .... Perhaps this is because ....*

Plenary

Activity: Display some of the groups' findings. Ask the class what it shows. *What ideas did [names] investigate? What was the [most popular/second most popular/third most popular] idea? How many learners thought [idea 1] was the best idea? Do you agree?*

Suggested answers: Open. This will depend on the learners' ideas and preferences.

Reflection: Refer learners to the learning goals in their books (I can make a chart that shows children's ideas). See page xxiv for a suggested procedure.

Home learning ideas

Activity: Give learners a copy of downloadable 2.2 to use with their family at home, or they could make their own chart. They could use it to find out what the people in their family would like to see growing in their local area. They could then bring the chart back to school with their findings.

Home–school link: Explain that the children have been learning how to conduct a simple survey about what plants people would like to see in the local area. Ask parents/care givers if they could help their children to do a simple survey with a few family members or neighbours.

2.3 Where can I find more facts and ideas?

LEARNING OBJECTIVES: EVALUATION

1E.01 Evaluating sources: Select a source relevant to a given issue and explain reasons for choice

LEARNING GOALS

- I can choose a good source of facts and ideas about gardens

LEARNING ATTRIBUTES

This lesson gives learners the opportunity to be:

- Reflective as learners, developing their ability to learn

Resources needed

Learner's Skills Book pages 42–44

Downloadable 2.3 ('How to make a small vegetable garden')

Downloadable 2.4 ('A good garden for minibeasts')

Downloadable 2.5 ('A good garden for birds')

Downloadable 2.6 ('My favourite place')

Downloadable 2.7 ('What can I find out from my own source?')

Downloadable 2.8 (model dialogues)

A selection of books, magazines, catalogues or advertisements at a suitable level for the learners. Most should be relevant to the issue of constructing a garden. Some should be deliberately *not* relevant

Note: If you would like learners to make their own minibeast hotel, the sources below may help with instructions

Tŷ Pawb's guide for making your own bug hotel, available on their website.

Nature Play WA's DIY Bug Hotel guide, available on their website.

Starter

Good for: Activating learners' prior understanding of relevance.

Activity: Decide on a topic you have already studied with this class. Collect a selection of resources – for example, images or books. Some should have direct relevance to the topic. Some should be unrelated. Tell the learners that you want to find out about [name of topic] but you need their help. Hold each resource up in turn. Ask the learners *Will this help me to find out about [name of topic]?* Ask the learners to point to the window (or similar) if they think it will help. Ask the learners to point to the door (or similar) if they think it will not help.

Prior learning: It would be beneficial for learners to have had prior knowledge of different parts of a book – for example, *title page, contents and their functions.*

What do we need to find out?

Good for: Asking basic, relevant questions about a given issue.

Activity:

1 Explain that Sofia and her friends need to come up with questions to find out more about their garden idea. Show the learners the three possible questions. Ask them to select which question is most helpful to Sofia and her friends who want to grow butterfly-friendly plants. If your class needs additional context before attempting it you can display the dialogue (downloadable 2.8) and check understanding.

2 Prompt learners to remember their most popular idea from 1.2. Explain that it is a good idea to think of lots of questions, and then pick the best one. Put learners in pairs to share their ideas – point out the useful question words in the book (What, How, Where).

3 Get learners to record their best idea (in the book or in their notebook if they need more space).

Answers and formative assessment:

1 Check that the learners have correctly indicated that 'What plants do butterflies like?' is the best question.

2 Check that learners can write questions that are relevant to an idea they have developed for something to put/grow in a school garden.

Differentiation:

Give support by scaffolding a process of elimination. *Is Q1 about butterflies?* (No) *Is Q1 about plants?* (No) *Is this going to be the best question? Why?* Repeat this process. Establishing that 'What plants do butterflies like?' was the best question because it contained both parts, namely, plants and butterflies. Help the learners to unpick the different elements (or 'parts') of their ideas.

Give extra challenge by asking learners to suggest some ways that Sofia and the team could find out the answer to their question. Ask learners to explain their selection: *This is the best question because …*

What is a good source of information?

Good for: selecting a source relevant to a given issue and being able to explain reasons for choice

Activity:

1 Check that learners understand what Zara is trying to do – make a good garden that minibeasts will come and live in. (Note: we are using 'minibeasts' as a learner-friendly, non-scientific term that covers insects, spiders, worms and other very small creatures). Remind learners of the Starter activity. Explain that Zara is finding out ideas for a school garden just as Sofia is. Zara's idea for a garden is different. She wants all different kinds of minibeasts to make their home there. So she needs to come up with questions to find out how to make a school garden that has lots of minibeasts living in it. Tell learners to look at the four sources and decide whether or not each source will help Zara, drawing a star, smiley face or sad face to show their opinion.

2 Display the speech bubble and useful words, and demonstrate how to use the language to model how to talk about one of the four sources: *This is [a very good/quite a good/not a good] source because ....* Ask the learners to use the same language to explain their ideas to a partner.

Suggested answers:

1 'Cat facts': not a good source because it is not about gardens or minibeasts.

'The giant apple': not a good source because it is not about gardens or insects. (Learners might also point out that it is a storybook).

'Gardens for bees': a very good source. Bees are minibeasts, so it is about gardens and minibeasts.

The adult talking to learners: quite a good source. He is showing the learners some plants so he probably knows about plants. Maybe he knows about plants for minibeasts.

2 Can learners explain why each source is or is not a good source for Zara to use?

Differentiation:

Give support by restricting the choice initially to good/not good before considering quite/very. Display the model dialogue shown in downloadable 2.8 and work through the questions to check understanding.

Give extra challenge by giving learners several sources and asking them to put the sources in order from best to worst.

What can I find out from my own source?

Good for: Talking about information on a given issue in sources provided. Formative assessment of learners' understanding of how to select sources/parts of sources for use in investigating an issue.

Activity:

1 Supply a range of sources of varying relevance to the issue of creating a garden (e.g. books, magazines, pictures). Alternatively, give out copies of downloadables 2.3–2.6. Give learners time to select a source they consider suitable. When they have, ask them to explain why they think it is suitable either in writing or by explaining to you or their partner.

2 Display/focus on the table. Demonstrate how to decide which box a fact or idea belongs in by using some examples – for example, a bean plant (Good plants to grow), a seat (Good things to put in a garden), water the plants (Good things to do). Allow learners time to look at their chosen source and find ideas or information in the text or pictures, then draw and/or write them in the table (or on downloadable 2.7).

3 Model how to talk about things you found out using the language provided – for example, *I found out that a water lily is a good plant to grow in a pond.* Ask learners to talk to a partner about what they found out, or share ideas as a whole class.

Answers and formative assessment:

3 Learners' own answers.

Can learners tell you at least one relevant fact or idea that they have found in their chosen source?

Differentiation:

Give support by limiting the choice of resources. Choose resources at an appropriate level for the learners, and provide additional support by modelling reading strategies.

Give extra challenge by extending the choice of resources to less familiar items or plants. Ask the learners to explain their reasons for their choices *Why do you think that would be a good idea?* And to use the sources to explain their reasoning *What gave you that idea?*

Plenary

Activity: Repeat the Starter Activity, this time displaying resources that may or may not be relevant to the issue of creating a garden for a school. Ask selected learners to give a reason for which way they are pointing (see instructions for the Starter Activity).

Suggested answers: Open. Look for appropriate reasons that are based on the learners' understanding of relevance to the project.

Reflection: Refer learners to the learning goals in their books (I can choose a good source of facts and ideas about gardens). See page xxiv for a suggested procedure.

2.4 How can we make a model of a school garden?

LEARNING OBJECTIVES: COLLABORATION

1Cl.01 Working together: Work positively with others, sharing resources while working independently or with others

ADDITIONAL LEARNING OBJECTIVES

1A.04 Solving problems: Choose a possible solution to an issue from a range of actions given

1E.02 Evaluating perspectives and arguments: State an opinion about a given issue

LEARNING GOALS

- I can work with my group to make a model of a school garden

LEARNING ATTRIBUTES

This lesson gives learners the opportunity to be:

- Innovative and equipped for new and future challenges

Resources needed

Learner's Skills Book pages 45–47

Downloadable 2.8 (model dialogues)

Video 2

Materials for model making from the following:

- Construction materials: assorted junk modelling materials, plastic construction toys or wooden blocks, play people, nuts and bolts, straws and connectors, small wooden sticks (e.g. lolly sticks or twigs from a plant), paper straws.
- Cutting and joining resources: scissors, hole punches, glue, sticky tape, treasury tags, ribbon, split pins, wool, string.
- Stationery: paper, card, cardboard boxes, cardboard box lids, trays.
- Enhancements: buttons, threads, pom poms, wool, ribbon, stickers.
- For imaginative play: play people of an appropriate size for the learners' models.

Please ensure that all materials and tools are compliant with your school's health and safety policy.

Starter

Good for: Preparing learners to choose a possible solution to an issue from a range of actions given.

Activity: Show the learners the range of tools and materials that you have available for model building. Show an item (or an image of the item) that might be appropriate to put in a school garden. Say that you would like to make a model of it but that you need their help. Ask the learners to think which of the materials and tools they would use to make a model of that item. Allow some time for think–pair–share.

Prior learning: It is beneficial if learners have had prior experience of creating designs and making models using simple tools and materials.

What kind of model garden will we make?

Good for: Understanding the range of possible solutions.

Activity:

1 Explain to the learners that they will be working with their group to make a model of the kind of garden that they would like to have for their school. First, they will look at the photos of gardens, which will help them with ideas. Go through the questions and, to further support, you can play the video. 

2 Ask learners to compare answers in pairs, then take feedback as a class.

3 Watch the video again and answer the question. Have a class discussion and draw out connections between the different forms of the gardens and what people can do in them.

Suggested Answers: All the activities are possible except perhaps playing football.

What ideas from the video can learners use in their own model garden? Look for ideas that are appropriate to your school and possible to model.

Differentiation:

Give support by playing the video several times through. Focus the learners on one question each time. Pause the video at relevant points and repeat the question.

Give extra challenge by asking learners to explain which of the ideas they have seen would be best for their school and why, and which ideas might not work. Ask the learners to explain their selection or rejection of ideas by referring to their practicality and/or how they might suit the needs of different people using the garden.

What things will we put in our model garden?

Good for: Refining learners' ideas for their model garden.

Activity:

1 Support learners with making a plan for their model garden, using the form provided. Draw attention to the 'My idea' sections: learners do not necessarily have to go for the ideas suggested.

2 Read Arun's speech bubble with the learners. Use it as a model for learners to talk to a partner about what they would like.

Draw attention to the Did You Know? box. The information about making compost can be used in conjunction with the photo of a compost box in the 'Things in our garden' section of the model garden plan. You could, if you wished, make a compost box with the learners. This could be used as part of a scientific investigation into planting seeds in different conditions. (e.g. PBS's guide for making a composter).

Answers and formative assessment: Open. Look for ideas that are appropriate to the space that the school has available.

Your observation of learners' decisions while selecting appropriate ideas for their model will reveal learner attainment of problem solving skills. Are learners able to identify an appropriate solution during class discussions?

Differentiation:

Give support by working through the model dialogue (downloadable 2.8) in which the characters discuss what they would like to put in their model garden. Ask the learners which ideas they would like.

Give extra challenge by asking learners to refer back to what they put in their 'Things to do in our garden' section to check if there's anything else they need to include to make their chosen activities possible.

How should we work together?

Good for: Reinforcing expectations about working positively with others and then creating a model together.

Activity:

1 Remind learners about your expectations of appropriate conduct in class. Take some suggestions about suitable rules for working together and being fair with the resources. Learners write their favourite rule in their book; you could also make a list of class rules together to display for everyone to see.

2 Put learners into groups – make it clear that each group are making one model together, to include all the group members' ideas. Allow learners time to make their model garden (and to clear up afterwards).

Make sure that the learners have time to engage in imaginative play with their model gardens using play people. A diverse range of play people can be used to stimulate imaginative play that focuses on how the garden meets the needs of different people.

Answers and formative assessment: Open. Look for examples of learners adopting appropriate ways of working that contribute to producing an effective shared team outcome.

Differentiation:

Give support by demonstrating some possible ways of realising learners' ideas using the tools and materials you have available.

Give extra challenge by identifying challenges that other learners are facing and asking learners to offer helpful ideas and solutions to the problems faced by the other members of the team.

Plenary

Activity: Put the model gardens on display and ask learners to reflect on the processes involved in creating them. *What did you do? How did you work with your team? What kind of garden did your group want to make? How will different people enjoy your garden?*

Suggested answers: Open. Look for answers where learners identify how they worked and how this contributed to the end artefact: *We shared the pom poms. All the tops of the trees are nice. You can sit in the shade.*

Reflection: Refer learners to the learning goals in their books (I can work with my group to make a model of a school garden). See page xxiv for a suggested procedure.

Home learning ideas

Activity: Learners could make another model of a garden for their community and bring it in (or take a photo of it to bring in). Alternatively, they could draw a picture if modelling materials are not available.

Home–school link: Suggest appropriate 'junk modelling' material that can be used. Ask parents to help collect materials and talk about ideas with the learners. Alternatively, ask parents to talk about designs that their learners have drawn.

2.5 How can we tell other children about our model?

LEARNING OBJECTIVES: COMMUNICATION

1Cm.01 Communicating information: Answer questions with relevant information about a given issue

1Cm.02 Listening and responding: Listen to others in class discussions and respond with simple questions

LEARNING GOALS

- I can talk about our model gardens

LEARNING ATTRIBUTES

This lesson gives learners the opportunity to be:

- Engaged intellectually and socially, ready to make a difference

Resources needed

Learner's Skills Book pages 48–51

Downloadable 2.8 (Model dialogues)

Audio 6 with transcript of characters talking about their model gardens

The learners' models

Play people of an appropriate size

Starter

Good for: Activating learners' understanding of relevant questions.

Activity: Have the learners' model gardens out on display. Walk around the room and model noticing things and asking questions as the learners listen. *Oh look! I really like the way they have … in this model. I wonder how they …?* and so on. Give the learners time to look at other groups' models. Take some suggestions about things learners like or things they have questions about in the models they have looked at.

How can we tell other children about our model garden?

Good for: Preparing to answer questions with relevant information about a given issue.

Activity:

1 Focus attention on the picture of Sofia and Arun's model garden. Tell learners they are going to listen to the learners talking about their model. Ask them to read the list of things in the model garden, listen to Audio 6 and tick the items mentioned. *Which thing did they forget to talk about?* (The pond).

2 Read the questions in the Learners' Skills Book with the class. Play the audio again and ask them to talk about the answers to the questions with their partner.'

3 Ask the learners to think about what they will tell other learners about their model. Refer them to the 'Remember to:' box. Tell them to talk about each of the things in their garden – they should not forget something important like Sofia and Arun did. What will they say about each thing?

Give the learners time for imaginative play with their model using play people.

Answers and formative assessment:

2 a Sofia and Arun only made a small garden to fit the space they had. **b** They think their garden is a good place for people to relax.

When the learners are planning what to say about their garden, look for ideas that identify the intended use of specific garden features.

Differentiation:

Give support by providing a sentence scaffold based on the audioscript – for example, *We want lots of … in our garden. It's a really nice garden for people to ….*

Give extra challenge by asking learners to explain how their model garden meets different needs for different people/things – for example, learners, adults or wildlife.

What questions will we ask?

Good for: Preparing to ask relevant questions about a given issue.

Activity:

1 Learners decide which of Marcus's three questions are/are not useful for finding out about Sofia and Arun's garden.

2 Remind learners of what they noticed when looking at other groups' garden models during the Starter Activity. What would they like to find out more about? Ask learners to make up some good questions. They can use the useful question starters provided in the box if they wish: model some examples of how to use these. (e.g. What kind of plant is this?) Encourage learners to write down their questions in their notebooks so they remember them.

Answers and formative assessment:

1 'How old are you?' is the irrelevant question.

Can learners ask questions that are focused on features of the models that other groups have made?

Differentiation:

Give support by providing some examples of questions for the learners based on the models various groups have made.

Give extra challenge by asking learners to make up questions to find out how the other groups' model gardens meet different needs – for example, learners, adults or wildlife.

What can we find out from other children's models?

Good for: Listening to others in discussions and answering questions with relevant information.

Activity:

1 Divide the class into two groups. One half will go around the class asking the other learners about the models they have made. The rest will stay with their models to answer questions about their own model. Draw attention to the simple flowchart, which shows how they will be working. Allow time for learners to exchange questions and answers about some of the other groups' models, then swap roles.

2 Learners draw and/or write something they really liked in another group's garden model.

Answers and formative assessment: Can learners ask relevant questions to other learners about their garden? Can they ask relevant *follow-up* questions in response to the information other learners give them?

Differentiation:

Give support by modelling a conversation about a model garden using the dialogue in downloadable 2.8. Ask structured questions based on the dialogue before tackling the real models.

Give extra challenge by asking learners to report back on how the other groups' model gardens meet different needs.

Plenary

Activity: Ask learners to reflect on their favourite idea that they have seen in other learners' models using the useful language provided in the Useful Words box. Why did they like that idea so much?

Suggested answers: Open. Encourage learners to explain the reason why they have made that selection.

Reflection: Refer learners to the learning goals in their books (I can talk about our model gardens). See page xxiv for a suggested procedure.

Home learning ideas

Activity: Discuss the community garden models/pictures with family members.

Home–school link: Explain that learners have been talking to each other about their model school gardens. As parents/care givers, can they talk to learners about the model gardens/pictures that the learners made for the community? How will they meet the needs of different people and wildlife?

2.6 What have we learned?

LEARNING OBJECTIVES: REFLECTION

1Rf.03 Personal perspectives: Talk about what has been learned during an activity with support

1Rf.04 Personal learning: Talk about something liked in a particular activity

LEARNING GOALS

- I can talk about what I learned
- I can talk about something I liked

LEARNING ATTRIBUTES

This lesson gives learners the opportunity to be:

- Reflective as learners, developing their ability to learn

Resources needed

Learner's Skills Book pages 51–53

Downloadable 2.8 (model dialogues)

Downloadable 2.9 (enlarged version of 'Things I know now about gardens')

Starter

Good for: Activating learners' understanding of the various stages of the model garden project.

Activity: Explain that during this lesson, we are going to be thinking about all of the things that we have learned about during our garden project. Say that you need the learners' help to remember all of the things we did. *Did we make a model?* Point to the window (or similar) if you think 'yes'. Repeat this with a range of other activities that were/were not part of this project.

Explain that during this lesson, we are also going to be thinking about all of the things that we have enjoyed doing during our garden project.

What do I know now?

Good for: Structuring learners' identification of what has been learned during the model garden project.

Activity: Support learners in identifying facts or ideas they know now that they did not know before the project. Ask them to record these (through drawing and/or writing) in categories: plants, creatures, activities, furniture or features that they now know are good for/appropriate in gardens. The facts and ideas can include particular objects or plant types, for example, as well as any information about those things (e.g. You need to water plants/put them somewhere sunny, etc.; a pond might be good for frogs, etc.). You may wish to distribute copies of downloadable 2.9 for this.

Answers and formative assessment: Open. Look for appropriate responses that demonstrate understanding of different animals and plants that can inhabit garden environments, as well as things that people like to do.

Differentiation:

Give support by working through the model dialogue and questions (downloadable 2.8) with learners before they begin the task in the Learner's Skills Book.

Give extra challenge by asking learners to explain their responses. *[Name of plant] is a good plant to put in a garden because ….*

What did I enjoy doing?

Good for: Structuring learners' identification of what they enjoyed doing during the model garden project

Activity: Recall some of the things the class did during the project, using the small images as prompts. Ask learners to discuss whether they enjoyed the various activities and how much they enjoyed them using the useful language provided in the Useful Words box.

Answers and formative assessment: Open. Look for learners' responses that identify enjoyable aspects at different stages of the project.

Differentiation:

Give support by working through the model dialogue and questions in downloadable 2.8.

Give extra challenge by asking them to explain their responses, giving reasons. *[Activity] was a fun thing to do because …. … was my favourite thing to do because ….*

What have I learned how to do?

Good for: Structuring learners' identification of how their skills have developed during the model garden project

Activity: With the learners, read Arun's statement about what he has learned how to do. Following this model, learners identify and write a skill that they have developed.

Answers and formative assessment: Can learners identify a skill they have learned (as opposed to a fact)?

Differentiation:

Give support by working through the model dialogue and questions (downloadable 2.8). Use this to clarify the difference between learning a fact and learning a new skill.

Give extra challenge by asking learners to explain their responses, giving examples. *Before the garden project, I did not know how to [named skill]. Now I can [named skill] because I [activity described].*

Plenary

Activity: Share some effective responses to the last activity with the whole class.

Explain briefly what learners will be learning about in the next project that you will be working on and what the outcome of that project will be. Help them to break this process down. *What do you think we will need to do? What do you think we will need to find out? Who/what could help us?* Invite the learners to think about how what they have learned in this project (knowledge/skills/understanding) will help them to achieve the outcome for the next project.

Suggested answers: Open. Look for answers that demonstrate appropriate reflection on how learners' skills can be used in a different learning context.

Reflection: Refer learners to the learning goals in their books (I can talk about what I learned. I can talk about something I liked). See page xxiv for a suggested procedure.

Home learning ideas

Activity: Ask the learners to tell parents/care givers (and if appropriate extended family members) about their garden project. Suggest talking about what they have enjoyed and what they have learned.

Home–school link: Explain to parents/care givers that the garden project has now come to an end. Encourage them to ask their children questions about the things that they have enjoyed and skills that they have learned.

Taking it further

This unit has focused on what kinds of gardens *could* be created within the context of your school. A logical next step is to put some of the learners' proposals into practice – that is, to plant some plants in your school. What you can do realistically will depend on the nature and extent of the space you have available. It may be that the project can only extend as far as germinating some seeds within the classroom. Learners can still contribute their design ideas to decisions about how/where this takes place and what is sown, and they can observe the results.

Growing plants can be an excellent way to bring in expertise from the community your school serves. As has been noted elsewhere, all visits to school must of course be conducted within your school's safeguarding policy. Parents, extended family members and school employees could all be potential sources of expertise. Learners working with adults to realise garden projects can be an excellent way to promote inter-generational learning. The beauty of such learning is that it produces tangible results: some schools are able to supply their own kitchens with fresh produce grown onsite.

The design project included making plans to attract wildlife. Again, the nature and extent of wildlife that you would want to encourage in your school environment will depend on the space available and the local wildlife! The processes of making and placing bird feeders and bug hotels can open up rich learning opportunities: What are the best materials to use? How can we shape and fix these materials together? Where is the best place to put them? Which species will come and visit them? How can we record our observations? There is scope for potential development of this project right across the curriculum.

Learners who have successfully completed this project will have developed a range of skills and attributes which will enable them to attempt the Cambridge International Primary Global Perspectives Challenges 'Fun with fruits' and 'Looking after our world' with enhanced confidence.

› 3 What do we know about jobs?

Introduction

The structure of this project follows the structure of the previous project closely. For the most part, progression is provided by learners applying similar skills to a different and less familiar learning context. Progression can also be enhanced by reducing the extent of support (i.e. through scaffolding and modelling) and by moving learners to independent learning activities sooner.

Note that, as a key part of this project, you will need to arrange for a visitor to be interviewed by the learners. Although a visit in person would be preferable, you may be able to carry out the interview virtually (using appropriate technology). All visits should, of course, be conducted within the guidelines set out in your school safeguarding policy.

To begin with, in Getting Started, learners look at and discuss an image of a construction project in progress. Their discussion will build on their pre-existing understanding of the different jobs involved. Make a note of any misconceptions that emerge so that these can be addressed in due course. Learners should now have some experience of thinking about their own responses before opening up discussions in pairs/groups.

Learners ask questions about different jobs that people do (Lesson 1 Analysis). They consider their prior understanding of the world of work based on their own experience, and consider other learners' understanding as well as their own. Learners play a game that develops their ability to ask and answer questions (Lesson 2 Research). Then they focus on asking questions about the work somebody does; they are guided through this by first considering an imaginary scenario in which the book characters interview their own visitor (a welder). Learners move on to prepare questions for their 'real' visitor.

The learners deepen their understanding of appropriate sources of information by asking whether a given source is useful or not for their enquiry in a different context from previously (Lesson 3 Evaluation). Learners identify sources that will help them understand what tasks a particular job entails, who people who perform that role work with, and where their work takes place.

The learners use the knowledge and understanding gained of different jobs that people do to set up a role play (Lesson 4 Collaboration). They develop imaginative play to explore how different people work together in a given workspace.

They use their role play to tell other learners about their understanding of what happens in their workplace (Lesson 5 Communication). They then find out about what other learners have discovered. Following their study of other learners' role plays, they explain which ideas they think are most interesting to them personally.

Finally, learners reflect on what they have learned about the world of work (Lesson 6 Reflection). They are also asked to consider what new knowledge, skills and understanding they have developed with support. As with previous projects, they consider what aspects of the project they have enjoyed.

Cross-curricular links and themes.

This project lends itself particularly well to integration with theme-based learning on the world of work, including understanding the vital roles performed by adults who help them directly as part of their job.

The theme of different kinds of employment developed throughout this project builds understanding relevant to the UN Sustainable Development Goal 8: Promote sustained, inclusive and sustainable economic growth, full and productive employment and decent work for all.

Building understanding of the work that it is appropriate for adults to perform opens up opportunities to ensure that learners develop an understanding that they have the right to protection from work that is bad for their health or education. This fits with the UN Rights of the Child Article 32: Governments must protect children from economic exploitation and work that is dangerous or might harm their health, development or education. Governments must set a minimum age for children to work and ensure that work conditions are safe and appropriate.

Learners have opportunities to apply their knowledge and understanding of, and skills in:	
Reading skills	• Reading and listening to a range of work-themed books, drawing on background information and vocabulary provided • Making links from their reading to their own experiences of people at work in the local community • Demonstrating their understanding of explicit meaning in text provided in a role play area such as labels, lists and signage to find relevant information related to their work
Writing skills	• Writing simple information texts for use in their role play area such as labels, captions, lists, questions and instructions about how a particular job is done
Speaking and listening skills	• Listening to others (learners and adults) and responding appropriately • Asking and listening carefully to questions • Listening to and giving instructions • Engaging in imaginative play, enacting work roles and situations • Understanding that people speak in different ways and for different purposes in the workplace compared to in other contexts

Before beginning work on this project, it would be helpful if learners have knowledge of or have had previous experience of:

- Speaking to a group to share what they think about an experience
- Answering questions and explaining further when asked
- Understanding that people speak in different ways for different purposes
- Understanding that texts for different purposes look different – for example, use of photographs, diagrams and similar
- Recognising the different parts of a book – for example, title page, contents – and understanding their functions
- Taking part in imaginative play, acting out simple characters or situations

Assessment focus

The focus skills for this project are Collaboration, Reflection and Research. The following downloadables will support you with assessing learners' attainment against the curriculum framework:

- Downloadable 3.9 (Assessment guidance sheet: Collaboration)
- Downloadable 3.10 (Assessment record sheet: Collaboration)
- Downloadable 3.11 (Assessment guidance sheet: Reflection)
- Downloadable 3.12 (Assessment record sheet: Reflection)
- Downloadable 3.13 (Assessment guidance sheet: Research Part 2)
- Downloadable 3.14 (Assessment record sheet: Research Part 2)

For a general introduction to the approach to assessment in this course, see page xxiii

Getting started

Good for: Activating learners' prior understanding of work – what it is for and different people's perspectives on it.

Activity:

1 Focus on the picture and ask learners what kind of place this is (a building site). Draw attention to the five construction workers. Explain that the learners will be finding out more about the different kinds of work that people do throughout this project so that they can put on their own role play.

Ask the learners to name as many of the things in the picture as they can. Support them by providing any vocabulary they need.

2 Introduce the learners to the chant 'This is the way we build a home'. Read the words together first, providing support with vocabulary. Repeat the chant with Audio 7. Alternatively, these words can be sung to the tune 'Here we go round the mulberry bush.' Whichever method you use, please note that the verse is repeated. Ask the learners to choose one of the workers and practise miming what they are doing. Repeat the chant, this time asking learners to mime the actions of their chosen worker as they sing or chant.

Talk/ask about the picture using the suggested question 'What are these people making?' Allow the discussion to build on elements of the learners' own experiences. Give time for learners to think about their own responses before opening up discussions in pairs/ groups.

- Make sure that the learners understand that a building site is not a safe place for learners to play. The workers are specially trained and have protective equipment to keep them safe. Ask learners what the workers are wearing to keep them safe (hard hats to protect their heads and hi-vis vests so the people operating the machines can see them easily).
- Point out the worker kneeling by a partly built wall, laying bricks with a trowel. *What is she doing? Why is this an important job? Who is helping her? How?*
- *What other jobs are the construction workers doing? What are they building with? What tools/ machines are they using?* Have the learners ever seen workers doing jobs like this? Where?
- Point out the worker who is consulting a set of plans. *What is on the plans? Why is this an important job too?*

Answers and formative assessment: Open. This will depend on the learners' prior experience and their interests. It is useful for the rest of the project to bring out the following points:

- Different workers perform different tasks. All of these tasks help to achieve the same end goal.
- Work often involves moving and shaping materials using tools and/or machines.
- Workers often need to use special skills. These skills have to be learned.
- Workers often wear special clothes. In the case of the builders, this is to keep them safe as they work. Workers also wear special clothes if they are working with food.
- People work to provide money so that they can support themselves and their families.

Differentiation:

Give support by providing images of construction work that has taken/is taking place in your local area, or that is familiar to learners from the media. Ask learners to describe the work that they can see in these images prior to looking at the image on the Learner's Skills Book page.

Give extra challenge by providing images of construction work that has taken/is taking place in a less familiar context. Ask learners to discuss what work is being done, who is doing the work, what they need to do their job successfully, how they are helping each other and how each worker contributes differently to the same end goal.

3.1 What work do people do?

LEARNING OBJECTIVES: ANALYSIS

1A.01 Identifying perspectives: Say something known about an issue

LEARNING GOALS

- I can talk about different jobs that people do

LEARNING ATTRIBUTES

This lesson gives learners the opportunity to be:

- Confident in working with information and ideas – their own and those of others

Resources needed

Learner's Skills Book pages 56–58

Audio 8 with transcript of Jack, Emily and Shreya talking about their jobs

Starter

Good for: Formative assessment of learners' understanding of the world of work. Learners who consistently point appropriately may well need further challenge during the lesson. Learners who consistently point incorrectly may well need additional support during the lesson.

Activity: Tell the learners that in this project, we will be finding out all about the different kinds of jobs that people do for a living. Name an activity – for example, building a house. *Is this something that people would do as part of their work? Point to the window if you think 'yes' Point to the door if you think 'no'. Point to the ceiling if you think 'maybe'.* Repeat with a range of jobs that the learners might be familiar with as a result of seeing them in the local area. Choose some (e.g. 'relaxing in the garden') that are almost certainly not work tasks and some that could be done for leisure *or* professionally (e.g. playing football). If learners are unsure, remind them that when people go out to work, they earn money. This supports them and their families.

Where do people work?

Good for: Learners to gain confidence in talking about the different kinds of work that people do. Formative assessment of the learners' level of prior understanding.

Activity: Ask learners to work with a partner. They should look at the photos of people at work in the Learner's Skills Book and discuss the five questions together. Take feedback as a class.

Make sure that learners are clear about what a factory is: a building where several people work together to make things (often with machines). Can they think of any other things that might be made in a factory?

Answers and formative assessment:

1 a Kitchen (photo 1); factory (photo 3); boat (photo 4); office (photo 2).

b Cook/chef (photo 1); car worker (photo 3); fisher/fisherman (photo 4); office worker (photo 2).

c (Accept answers based on what is in the photos or what the learners already know). Oven, other kitchen utensils (photo 1); a machine to lift up the car, various kinds of tools (photo 3); boat, fishing pots or nets, flags and buoys to show where the nets are (photo 4); computer, desk (photo 2).

d Hair net (photo 1); no special clothes in photo 2– although you could discuss that sometimes factory workers wear overalls, or goggles to protect their eyes; long waterproof trousers, a woolly hat (to keep them warm), waterproof boots (photo 4); no special clothes for photo 2.

e Open. Look for places appropriate to the jobs identified.

Can learners use their prior understanding and visual clues in the photos to answer the questions?

Differentiation:

Give support by modelling a discussion based on the first image. *Oh look, I wonder where this person is working? Can it be a building site? No, it can't be a building site because I can't see any bricks.*

Give extra challenge by asking learners about how the tools or clothes used by each worker are appropriate to their use – for example, *Why does the baker need an oven?*

What different kinds of jobs do people do?

Good for: Building understanding that people work in different places in different ways and that they use different tools to help them.

Activity:

1 Explain to the learners that they are going to hear people talking about their work: draw attention to the photos of Jack, Emily and Shreya. Ask them to look at the pictures that we can see of three workplaces, and ask how they are different from each other. Point out and check understanding of the three workplace names (office, factory and building site). Explain the matching task, demonstrating how to draw a line from the photograph of the person to the name of the workplace. Then ask learners to listen to each person talking about where they work (play audio 8). Check answers.

2 Now explain the sentence completion task before learners listen to the audio again.

3 Explain that Sofia is doing a project about different jobs that people do and would like to know who would be best to answer her question. Give learners time to discuss this in pairs.

4 In pairs again, learners consider which of the three workers they would like to interview. As a class, review and discuss the questions that the learners came up with.

Answers and formative assessment:

1 Office [3] Factory [2] Building site [1].

2 Jack helps to make chocolate; Emily is helping to build a tower block; Shreya helps people to fix computers.

3 Emily.

4 Open. This will depend on learners' interests.

Listen carefully to learners' suggestions for Question 4. Are they able to come up with a question that is *relevant* – one that is useful to the task of finding out about jobs, and appropriate to finding out more about the worker they have chosen?

Differentiation:

Give support by modelling a process of elimination. Pick out the key information in the audio clip by pausing at relevant times. *Who is this? Does Jack work in an office?* (No) *Does Emily?* (No) *So who must work in an office?*

Give extra challenge by asking learners to complete extended sentences for each worker: *[Name] works in .... He/She lives in .... At work he/she wears.... At work he/she uses....*

For Question 4, challenge learners to think of a different question for each of the three workers.

Who works near where I live?

Good for: Learners to activate their prior understanding of work that takes place in the local community.

Activity: Learners draw a person that they have seen doing their job near their home or school. They discuss their drawing with a partner using the questions provided for guidance.

Answers and formative assessment: Open. Encourage learners to include in their drawings as much relevant visual context as they can about where they work and how they do their job.

Have they been able to identify a local worker that they have seen, and have they been able to describe the work that person does, in simple terms?

Differentiation:

Give support by encouraging learners to draw someone at work within school, if they genuinely struggle to show understanding of any work outside school, for example, the school receptionist or site staff.

Give extra challenge by asking learners to explain what they think the reasons are why the person they have drawn wears certain protective clothes or how they make use of certain tools or machines as part of their work.

Plenary

Activity: Display some learners' drawings together with the questions. Give the learners time for think–pair–share and invite some responses.

Give the learners time to look at some of the other learners' drawings. Ask them to answer the questions based on what they can see. Can they talk about some different jobs that people do?

Answers: Open.

Reflection: Refer learners to the learning goals in their books (I can talk about different jobs that people do). See page xxiv for a suggested procedure.

Home Learning ideas

Activity: Ask learners to look around on their journey to and from school and spot people who are working. Follow this up in class. Ask them who they have seen working. Were they working alone or with someone else? What were they doing and why?

Home–school link: Explain to parents/care givers that the learners are starting a project about the different kinds of work that people do. Ask parents to help children notice different kinds of work that people are doing when they are out and about together. Ask parents to talk to their children about what these workers are doing and why.

3.2 How can I find out about jobs?

LEARNING OBJECTIVES: RESEARCH

1Rs.01 Constructing research questions: Ask basic questions about a given issue

1Rs.02 Information skills: Talk about information on a given issue in sources provided

1Rs.03 Conducting research: Begin to participate in simple investigations and ask basic questions to find information and opinions

LEARNING GOALS

- I can ask questions about jobs

LEARNING ATTRIBUTES

This lesson gives learners the opportunity to be:

- Responsible for themselves, responsive to and respectful of others

Resources needed

Learner's Skills Book pages 59–61

Audio 9 of people talking about their jobs.

Plain white headbands (one per group of four learners) and sticky notes with a range of job titles written on them

Invite a visitor to your class to talk about their job (check your school's safeguarding policy and make sure that the visitor understands it. Follow your school's policy throughout the process). Ideally the visitor should be someone who is able to give the learners information about a job that could form the basis of a successful role play later in the project.

Starter

Good for: Activating learners' prior understanding of different kinds of work.

Activity: Display pictures of workers doing a range of different jobs that are likely to be familiar to the learners in your setting. Ensure that they are visible to all the learners. Label each picture with the relevant job title – for example, nurse, bus driver, baker. Tell learners you are going to say something about this person's job and they should point to who they think you are referring to. Start with a description that could apply to more than one – for example, *This worker makes things/helps people* (or similar). Provide further clues until it is apparent which worker you are referring to. If you wish to continue this activity, invite a learner to select a picture and provide clues. It might be a good idea to have them whisper who it is so that you can check that their clues are correct.

What questions can I ask about jobs?

Good for: Building skills that are used in simple investigations and asking basic questions to find information.

Activity:

1 Show the learners how the characters in the book are playing a game. Check understanding by asking learners which character is trying to work out what his job is (Marcus) and who can answer his questions (the others).

Play Audio 9. In the recording, the characters are playing the game whereby questions can only be answered 'yes' or 'no'. Ask learners to tell you what was wrong with Marcus's second question (it cannot be answered by a simple 'yes' or 'no').

Check understanding of how Marcus correctly arrived at the conclusion that he was a builder (he wears a hard hat and uses bricks).

Ask learners to recap the questions that Marcus asked.

2 Have learners work in pairs or small groups to think of three more questions that they would like to ask. Draw attention to the useful question starters.

3 Learners can then play the game in their own groups. Check that the 'hat wearers' understand what their job is before you start the game.

4 When every learner has had a chance to be the 'hat wearer', ask all learners to write down the name of the job that was on their own hat and a good question that they asked.

Answers and formative assessment: Open. Can learners ask appropriate questions and use their understanding to narrow down possible occupations?

Differentiation:

Give support by repeating the audio and discussing what Marcus could have been thinking at each stage. Play another round with you trying to guess what job you are. Model your thought process out loud – for example, *Oh, so I don't work in a fire station, that means I can't be a fire fighter. What shall I ask next? I know: Do I wear any special clothes?*

Give extra challenge by providing a more challenging range of jobs, including some less familiar to the learners in their daily experience of the local area.

How can I talk to someone about their job?

Good for: Forming a question that is suitable for a simple investigation to find both information and opinions.

Activity:

1 Talk about why Arun, Marcus, Sofia and Zara are excited, and check that the learners understand that the characters are expecting a visitor who does a particular job (a welder). Read the Did You Know? box together.

One possible way that you could enrich this activity would be by performing yourself 'in role' as the welder. To do this successfully, you would need to do some research first! In this way, you could help the learners to practise what to do in a question-and-answer situation.

Before learners look at the characters' questions, clarify what is meant by the term 'opinion' by asking learners to choose 'fact' or opinion' for a series of statements – for example, *Apples grow on trees* (Fact); *Apples are delicious* (Opinion). Then move on to more work-related statements – for example, *A welder uses a special tool to join pieces of metal* (Fact); *Welding is a really interesting job* (Opinion). Read through the questions with the learners. Check whether they can identify which questions are about facts and which is about an opinion.

2 Put learners in pairs to come up with a further relevant question for the welder. Take suggestions and write them on the board. Can the class identify which ones are about facts and which are about opinions?

3 Divide the learners into groups. Each group firstly discusses ideas for workers that they would like to invite to school to talk about their jobs. (You may wish to restrict this choice to those who, realistically, you would be able to invite in to school to talk about the work that they do).

4 Explain that it is a good idea to prepare questions in advance prior to a visitor coming in. We want to find out two kinds of information: facts about the job; the person's opinions – for example, what they find satisfying or challenging.

Answers and formative assessment:

1 The question 'What is the best thing about your job?' is about an opinion, while the other questions are about facts.

Can learners devise relevant questions that ask about both facts and opinions?

Differentiation:

Give support by rereading the characters' questions with the learners before they start on their own discussion. Clarify the difference between a 'fact' question (e.g. *What time do you have to leave home?*) and an opinion focused one (e.g. *How did you feel when you got the job?*)

Model some questions that you might use for a slightly different visitor. Choose an example close enough so that some but not all of the questions would be appropriate.

Give extra challenge by asking learners to construct a mixture of closed questions (one- or two-word answers) and open ones (those that would require a longer answer).

What did the visitor tell us?

Good for: Conducting an investigation that looks at facts and opinions and summarising the findings.

Activity:

1 Make sure you have reminded the learners about appropriate behaviour when a visitor is in class. Remind them of how you did the interview when you took on the role of the welder (if you chose to do this).

Learners conduct their interview with your visitor. Remind them to use the questioning process you agreed with them. If possible, record the interview so you can replay parts of it later.

2 Afterwards, discuss with the learners what they have found out. Ask them to record something they have found out from the visitor in their book.

Answers and formative assessment: Open. Check that learners ask questions that elicit both factual information and opinions.

Differentiation:

Give support by having learners practise asking their prepared questions before they interview the visitor.

Give extra challenge by challenging them to draw some possible simple conclusions from the answers. *The best part of the job is … Perhaps this is because …*

Plenary

Activity: If possible, play back a section of the interview. Ask the class questions that are relevant to that section – for example, *What facts did we learn? What opinions did [the visitor] give? What do you think was the most interesting thing we found out here? Would you like to do this job?*

Suggested answers: Open. Check understanding of facts/opinions is secure.

Reflection: Refer learners to the learning goals in their books (I can ask questions about jobs). See page xxiv for a suggested procedure.

Home learning ideas

Activity: Ask learners to find out about a different job by talking to a family member or another adult (with parental approval and supervision). Alternatively, learners could visit a library to find out about a different job. You could allocate a section of classroom display space to put up learners' drawings and/or writing which conveys what they have discovered.

Home–school link: Explain that the learners have been learning how to conduct an interview with someone to find out about their work. Ask parents/care givers if they could help learners to conduct an interview with a family member or neighbour about the work that they do. Alternatively, visit a local library and see what information they have available.

3.3 Where can I find out more about jobs?

LEARNING OBJECTIVES: EVALUATION

1E.01 Evaluating sources: Select a source relevant to a given issue and explain reasons for choice

1E.02 Evaluating perspectives and arguments: State an opinion about a given issue

LEARNING GOALS

- I can choose a good source of facts and ideas about jobs
- I can give my opinion about what I have found out

LEARNING ATTRIBUTES

This lesson gives learners the opportunity to be:

- Reflective as learners, developing their ability to learn

Resources needed

Learner's Skills Book pages 62–65

Downloadable 3.1 ('What can I find out from my own source?' table)

Downloadable 3.2 (model answer for 'What can I find out from my own source?' table)

Downloadable 3.3 ('How a baker makes naan bread')

Downloadable 3.4 ('What does a welder do?')

Downloadable 3.5 ('We all help to make a jumper')

Downloadable 2.8 (model dialogues from Project 2 as guidance)

A selection of books at a suitable level for the learners

A selection of images of people at work (including one specifically for the Starter Activity)

A list of questions for the Starter Activity (some relevant to the Starter Activity image, some unrelated)

Starter

Good for: Reactivating learners' prior understanding of relevance.

Activity: Show an image of a person doing a job that is familiar to the learners you are teaching. Say that you want to find out about the job that this person does, but you need the learners' help. Display and read together some pre-prepared questions. Some should be directly relevant to the job (e.g. for a pilot, *How did you learn to fly a plane?*; for a miner, *Is it very dark working under the ground?*) Other questions should be not relevant (e.g. *Can you ride a bicycle?*). Ask the learners *Will this question help me to find out about this job?* Ask the learners to point to the window (or similar) if they think it will help. Ask the learners to point to the door (or similar) if they think it will not help.

What is the best source of information?

Good for: Selecting a source relevant to a given issue and explaining reasons.

Activity:

1 Explain that Arun and his friends have each chosen a job that they would like to find out more about. Show the learners the four possible sources of information. Establish why the book 'Building a Ship' is most helpful to Arun, who wants to find out about the work that a welder does.

2 Learners then identify a job that they would like to find out more about. You may wish to encourage them to choose jobs that you have good sources of information about.

Introduce the learners to the idea that they will be doing a role play later in the project. The more information they have about what happens in the workplace they choose, the better role play they will be able to do. What kind of workplace would they like to act out? A factory? A building site? An office? Take some suggestions. Organise the learners into groups (for their role play preparation and for the role play itself). You could group learners using a range of criteria: learners who are interested in similar jobs, learners with different levels of prior attainment. Alternatively, you may wish to simply allocate jobs to groups you have already established for other curriculum study.

Learners record their chosen job in their book.

Answers and formative assessment: Are learners able to identify whether a source is relevant or not? If they pick the correct source, can they explain why this source is relevant?

1 Arun 1; Zara 4; Marcus 2; Sofia 3

Differentiation:

Give support by scaffolding the process of elimination further. *What job does Marcus want to find out about?* (A baker) *do bakers build houses?* (No) and so on. Provide a dialogue similar to the dialogues in Project 2 (downloadable 2.8). Have the characters discuss a job that they would like to find out more about and provide structured questions to guide learners' understanding.

Give extra challenge by asking learners to explain their reasons. *Why is this book helpful for [name of character]? What kind of worker would they like to be in their role play? Why?*

What do we need to find out?

Good for: Devising a question relevant to a given issue.

Activity:

1 Check that learners understand what Marcus is trying to do – find out about the work that a baker does. Remind learners of the Starter Activity. Explain that Marcus has been thinking of questions too. He has found a good question to ask about the work a baker does.

2 Explain to the learners that they should think of questions to ask about the job that they have selected for their role play. Make sure that they are in the group that they will be working with to perform the role play and double check they understand what their job is.

3 Learners record their favourite question in their book.

Formative assessment: Can learners come up with questions relevant to what they need to find out?

Differentiation:

Give support by suggesting a limited choice of jobs for the learners to ask questions about. This could be restricted to: jobs that learners are more familiar with, jobs for which you have directly relevant sources of information available or jobs that would more easily lend themselves to being performed successfully in a class role play.

Give extra challenge by suggesting a wider choice of jobs for the learners to ask questions about. This could be widened to include ones they are less familiar with/ ones for which you have fewer directly relevant sources of information available/ones which would be more challenging to represent in a class role play.

What can I find out from my own source?

Good for: Talking about information on a given issue in sources provided.

Activity:

1 Supply a range of sources of varying relevance to the issue of work (e.g. books, pictures, video clips, etc.). Alternatively, give out copies of downloadables 3.3–3.5. Give learners time to select a source they consider suitable.

Display/focus on the table in the book. Model the process of deciding which box a fact or idea belongs in by using the worked example in downloadable 3.2. Give learners time to look for information about their chosen job and find ideas/ information in the text or pictures, then draw and/ or write them in the table or on downloadable 3.1 'What can I find out from my own source?'

2 Model how to talk about things you find interesting using the language provided – for example, *In my opinion, the most interesting thing I found out was …* Ask learners to talk to a partner/their group about what they found interesting and then share ideas as a whole class.

Answers and formative assessment:

2 Learners' own answers. Can learners tell you at least one relevant fact or idea that they have found in their chosen source?

Differentiation:

Give support by working with the learners to break the task down into stages: sorting out the information into helpful/not helpful, locating relevant images/text, recording the relevant information in the right place, and so on.

Give extra challenge by asking the learners to explain their reasons for their choice of 'most interesting fact'. *Why do you think that was the most interesting fact? How could you use this in your role play?*

Plenary

Activity: Share some interesting facts that the learners have found out. Select ones that you think lend themselves well to being performed in a role play – for example, suggestions about appropriate clothing, actions that could be performed or tools that could be used. Provide some suggestions for how they could be acted out. Then share another interesting fact with the learners and ask for their help (e.g. *Car workers sometimes use robots to help them make the cars. How could we show this with actions?*) Give time for think–pair–share.

Answers and formative assessment: Open. Look for appropriate justifications – especially those that are based on the learners' understanding of relevance to the role play project. Learners may find it appropriate to perform their suggestions.

Reflection: Refer learners to the learning goals in their books (I can choose a good source of facts and ideas about jobs. I can give my opinion about what I have found out). See page xxiv for a suggested procedure.

3.4 How can we do a role play about work?

LEARNING OBJECTIVES: COLLABORATION

1Cm.01 Working together: Work positively with others, sharing resources while working independently or with others

ADDITIONAL LEARNING OBJECTIVES

1A.04 Solving problems: Choose a possible solution to an issue from a range of actions

LEARNING GOALS

- I can do a role play about work with my group

LEARNING ATTRIBUTES

This lesson gives learners the opportunity to be:

- Innovative and equipped for new and future challenges

Resources needed

Learner's Skills Book pages 66–71

Downloadable 3.6 ('Our work plan' – completed model)

Downloadable 3.7 ('Our work plan' – table for learners to complete)

Video 3 about how chocolate is made

Dressing up clothes, props, play equipment that can be used in flexible ways appropriate to the workplaces that the learners have researched

Printed safety signs and equipment (alternatively, the learners' own drawn/painted versions)

Modelling resources: boxes, plastic bottles, sticky tape, plastic hoops/cones, and so on

You will need to have either **a** a role play corner available that each group can use in turn or **b** a large enough clear space in which each group can set up their role play alongside the other groups' 'workplaces'

Starter

Good for: Preparing learners to choose a possible solution to an issue from a range of actions given.

Activity: Show the learners an item from the range of costumes and play equipment that you have available for role play – for example, a hi-viz vest. Show an image of a workplace where it would be appropriate – for example, a building site. Say that you would like to do a role play about that workplace but need their help. *Would a [e.g. hi-viz vest] be good for a [e.g. building site] role play?* Establish that it would. Ask the learners which of the other items they could use in a role play about that workplace. Which would not be appropriate? Allow time for think–pair–share. Repeat with other workplaces and other items.

What different jobs do people do in a workplace?

Good for: Understanding a range of possible solutions available.

Activity:

1 Explain to the learners that they will be working with their group to set up a role play. In this role play space, they will act out the job that they have researched. First, they will watch the video to help them with ideas for their own workplace. You can also point out how, in one kind of workplace (a chocolate factory), many different tasks are performed. This will help them with ideas for their own workplace. Go through the questions and play the video.

Ask learners to compare answers in pairs, then take feedback as a class.

2 Read through the second set of questions, explaining the word 'mould' with reference to the Did You Know? box. Play the video.

Ask who put the chocolate in boxes (the robot arm). *How did the robot arm know how to pack chocolate?* Establish that a worker has to *operate* or *program* the robot arm to make it work.

3 Ask learners to act out tasks that they have seen the workers performing with a partner. In discussion, draw out parallels between the way different tasks

are performed by different people in a chocolate factory and the different tasks that they will want to demonstrate in their own role play about the workplace they have researched. Point out and discuss the very clean clothing and hair covers (why do learners think these are necessary?)

Answers and formative assessment:

1 **a** in a chocolate factory; **b** to populate from video; **c** to populate from video; **d** to populate from video

2 All the listed jobs are in the video except 'Eating the chocolate'.

What ideas from the video can learners use in their own workplace role play? Look for ideas that are appropriate to the work that they will perform. Can the learners identify possible ways to act the task out?

Differentiation:

Give support by playing the video several times through. Focus the learners on one question each time. Pause the video at relevant points and repeat the question. If learners find drawing parallels between the chocolate factory and a different workplace challenging, consider setting up a chocolate factory scenario as your workplace role play.

Give extra challenge by asking learners to explain ways in which they could adapt working practices seen in the chocolate factory to their own role play. Ask the learners to explain their selection or rejection of costume/prop ideas by referring to similarities and differences between the two places of work.

What things will we do in our role play?

Good for: Refining learners' ideas for their role play.

Activity:

1 Use Arun's speech bubble to remind learners of the task. Encourage them to use the same language modelled in the speech bubble to talk about their own plans for their workplace and role play: Our workplace will be a [building site, hospital, etc.]. We will pretend to [build houses, look after sick people, etc.].

2–4 Support learners with making a plan for their workplace role play. They should work with a partner/their group to list the jobs they will do in their workplace, any special clothing (and footwear, head coverings etc.) they may need, and any other items they will use.

Answers and formative assessment: Open. Check whether learners can choose appropriate tasks to perform in their role play (i.e. relevant to their chosen workplace). Look for ideas that are appropriate to the space that the school has available.

Check whether they can explain why they need particular clothing or other items.

Differentiation:

Give support by working through the model work plan in downloadable 3.6 in which the characters identify what role each member of the team will take on and how they will perform their role. Ask the learners which tasks they would like to act out. What props/costumes will they use to help them perform successfully? Provide them with plausible alternatives to choose from if they find it challenging to suggest their own.

Give extra challenge by asking learners to suggest how they could help other members of their group to create their ideas when they come to performing the role play. It might be helpful to refer learners back to what they put in their 'Things to do in our garden' section in Project 2 (section 2.3), which uses similar skills. Ask them to check if there's anything else they need to include to make their chosen activities possible.

How can we work together?

Good for: Setting expectations about working positively by dividing tasks with others appropriately.

Activity: Remind learners about your expectations of working together as part of a team. Emphasise that during discussion about the video, we understood that everyone's job was important so everyone had the tools/equipment that they needed. Take some suggestions about suitable approaches to working together in a role play.

Put learners into their groups – make it clear that they are creating a role play of a single workplace together and should include all the group members' ideas.

1 Look at the characters' plan together (the full version is on downloadable 3.6). Ask questions to make sure learners understand the plan (What job will Zara do? Who will fix the wheels on? etc.) Allow learners time to plan their own role play together. (Give out copies of downloadable 3.7).

2 As each learner decides on their own job in the role play, ask them to draw a picture to show what they will be doing. A column is provided for this.

When the learners have set up their role play area, make sure that they have time to engage in imaginative play there.

Answers and formative assessment: Open. Look for examples of learners adopting appropriate ways of working that contribute to producing an effective group performance.

Differentiation:

Give support by demonstrating some possible ways that learners could use the available costumes, props and so on in their role play.

Give extra challenge by asking learners to offer helpful ideas and solutions to problems faced by the other members of their team.

Plenary

Activity: Ask one group to perform their role play to the class. It might be helpful to do this more than once. Ask learners to reflect on how the group worked together. What did they do? How did they work with their group? What kind of workplace did the group perform? How were different people involved?

Answers and formative assessment: Open. Look for answers where learners identify how they worked and how this contributed to the end role play. How did they make it as realistic as possible?

Reflection: Refer learners to the learning goals in their books (I do a role play about work with my group). See page xxiv for a suggested procedure.

Home learning ideas

Activity: Learners could engage in imaginative play about work at home (and maybe ask someone to take a photo of it to bring in). This could be with themselves in role or using 'small world' people in a model. Alternatively, they could draw a picture of themselves working in an imagined workplace and write about their imagined experience.

Home–school link: Suggest appropriate props and costume items that can be used if the learners want to create a role play at home. Ask parents to help collect materials for a role play and talk about ideas with the learners. Alternatively, ask parents to talk about the workplace scenarios that learners have drawn, written about and/or modelled.

3.5 How can we tell other children about our workplace?

LEARNING OBJECTIVES: COMMUNICATION

1Cm.01 Communicating information: Answer questions with relevant information about a given issue

1Cm.02 Listening and responding: Listen to others in class discussions and respond with simple questions

LEARNING GOALS

- I can talk about our workplace

LEARNING ATTRIBUTES

This lesson gives learners the opportunity to be:

- Engaged intellectually and socially, ready to make a difference

Resources needed

Learner's Skills Book pages 71–75

Downloadable 2.8 (model dialogues)

Audio 10 with transcript of characters' role play.

Roleplay items as in Lesson 3.4.

Starter

Good for: Activating learners' understanding of relevant questions.

Activity: Focus on one of the learners' prepared workplaces. Model noticing things and asking questions. *Ooh, look! I really like the way they have got … in this workplace. I wonder how they made it/what they are going to use it for*, and so on. Give the learners time to look at a different group's workplace. Take some suggestions about things learners would like to comment on or have questions about.

What shall we say in our role play?

Good for: Preparing to provide relevant information on a given issue.

Activity:

1 Focus attention on the picture of Sofia, Arun, Marcus and Zara's workplace. Ensure learners are familiar with the parts of the car that will be referred to in the listening task: wheels, pedals, dashboard. If necessary, pre-teach the word *operate*: you operate a piece of machinery (make it work). Tell learners they are going to listen to Arun, Sofia and Marcus talking about their role play. Ask the learners to read the list of jobs in the role play, listen to the audio and tick the items mentioned. Which jobs were not mentioned? (Putting in the seats).

2 Read the questions in the Learner's Skills Book with the learners. Play the audio again and ask them to talk about the answers to the questions with their partner.'

3 Ask the learners to think about what they will tell other learners about their workplace role play. Refer them to the Ideas box. Ask then to talk as a team about each of the jobs in their workplace, just as Arun, Sofia and Marcus did in the audio. What will they say about the work done by each member of the team?

Give the learners time for imaginative play in their workplace using the props and costumes.

Answers and formative assessment:

2 **a** Arun puts the wheels on; **b** Robots do some of the work in the factory; **c** He is working in an office next to the factory. He is buying parts for the cars over the phone.

When the learners are planning what to say about their workplace, look for ideas that identify the intended use of specific actions/costume/spoken words/props in recreating the workplace environment.

Differentiation:

Give support by providing a sentence scaffold based on the audioscript. For example, *Hello everyone. Welcome to our role play. Here is the … we made. We are …. My job was to …. Look, these are …. We made the … with …. I did …. It is like a real …*, and so on.

Give extra challenge by asking learners to explain how their role play shows the sequence of tasks carried out in a workplace (if that is relevant for their workplace). For example, *What happens first? Then what happens?*

What questions will we ask?

Good for: Preparing to ask relevant questions about a given issue.

Activity:

1 Learners decide which of the three questions are/are not useful for finding out about Sofia, Arun. Marcus and Zara's car factory

2 Based on the picture and the audio, learners suggest questions to ask the characters about their car factory. Support them with asking questions that are relevant.

Move on to thinking about the workplaces created by their own classmates. Remind learners of what they noticed when looking at costumes and props during the Starter Activity. What would they like to find out more about? Ask learners to make up some good questions, using the useful question starters provided in the box if they wish. Model some examples of how to use these (e.g. *How do you use the [named tool] in a [named workplace]?*) Encourage learners to write down their questions so they remember them.

Answers and formative assessment:

1 'What colour is the factory?' is the irrelevant question.

Can learners ask relevant questions that are focused on features of the role play workplaces that other groups have created?

Differentiation:

Give support by providing some examples of questions for the learners based on the workplace role plays that various groups have made.

Give extra challenge by getting learners to check that their own questions make sense and self-correct any that are unclear/irrelevant. Get learners to ask questions to find out how different workers each contribute to an overall aim. Encourage learners to make inferences based on things they can see in each workplace.

What can we find out from other children's role plays?

Good for: Listening to others and answering questions with relevant information.

Activity:

1 Give each group a turn to perform their own role play and watch another group. Each group will take it in turns to answer another group's questions about their role play, and to ask questions to another group. Draw attention to the simple flowchart, which shows how they will be working. Allow time for learners to exchange questions and answers, then swap roles.

2 Learners draw and/or write something they found particularly interesting in another group's role play.

Answers and formative assessment: Can learners ask relevant questions to other learners about their role play? Can they follow up with *further* questions in response to the information other learners give them?

Differentiation:

Give support by providing a model conversation about a workplace for the learners. Ask structured questions to guide their understanding. The conversation and questions about gardens in the 2.5 section of downloadable 2.8 provide an appropriate structure and can easily be adapted for use with this unit.

Give extra challenge by encouraging learners to say what was particularly good about another group's role play (e.g. the use of props, their acting, how they talked about it), and also how it could be improved further.

Plenary

Activity: Ask learners to reflect on the most interesting thing that they have seen in other learners' role plays. Why did they find that [action/idea] interesting? How did the other group inform them about what happened in their workplace successfully?

Answers and formative assessment: Encourage learners to explain the reason why they have made that selection. Look for the following in discussion: Can learners explain what they performed in their own role play? Can learners explain how other learners performed their role play? Can learners find out the purpose of the features included in other learners' role play scenarios?

Reflection: Refer learners to the learning goals in their books (I can talk about our workplace). See page xxiv for a suggested procedure.

Home learning ideas

Activity: Discuss the workplace role play with family members.

Home–school link: Explain that learners have been acting in role as workers in a workplace. As parents/care givers, can they talk to learners about the role play that they performed? Can they make a model of it at home or draw/write about it? Parents/care givers could talk about places where they have worked and the different jobs that people do there. Learners could (if appropriate) draw/model/role play what happens there.

3.6 What have we learned about jobs?

LEARNING OBJECTIVES: REFLECTION

1Rf.01 Personal contribution: Identify personal contribution in the form of an action intended to help achieve a shared outcome

1Rf.02 Teamwork: Identify an action that someone else contributed to achieve a shared outcome.

1Rf.03 Personal perspectives: Talk about what has been learned during an activity with support

1Rf.04 Personal learning: Talk about something liked in a particular activity

LEARNING GOALS

- I can talk about what I learned
- I can say what I did to help my group

LEARNING ATTRIBUTES

This lesson gives learners the opportunity to be:

- Reflective as learners, developing their ability to learn
- Responsible for themselves, responsive to and respectful of others

Resources needed

Learner's Skills Book pages 76–79

Downloadable 2.8 (model dialogue)

Downloadable 3.8 (enlarged version of 'Things I know now about jobs')

Starter

Good for: Activating learners' understanding of the various stages of the workplace role play project.

Activity: Explain that, during this lesson, we are going to be thinking about all of the things that we have learned about during our project all about work. Say that you need the learners' help to remember all of the things we did. 'Did we do a role play?' Point to the window if you think 'yes', and so on. Repeat with a range of other activities that were/were not part of this project. Explain that during this lesson, we are also going to be thinking about all of the things that we did to help our group during our project about different jobs that people do.

What do I know now?

Good for: Encouraging learners to reflect on what they have learned during the project.

Activity: Support learners in reflecting upon facts or ideas they know now that they did not know before the project. Ask them to record these in the table (through drawing and/or writing) in the categories provided. You may wish to distribute enlarged copies of downloadable 3.8 for this.

Answers and formative assessment: Open. Look for appropriate responses that demonstrate understanding of the nature of different workplaces, as well as identification/description of tasks that workers do based on the learners' research and experience of imaginative play in role as a worker.

Differentiation:

Give support by providing a model dialogue similar to the one provided in the 2.6 section of downloadable 2.8 entitled 'What did I enjoy doing?' and 'What did I learn how to do?' The structure is equally appropriate for this unit; however, you will need to adapt the content so that the characters talk about their workplace role play and so that the focus is on how they helped.

Give extra challenge by asking learners to develop their responses: *It is a good idea for a worker in a … to use a … because …*

How did I help my group?

Good for: Supporting learners as they reflect on their experience of collaborating during the project.

Activity:

1 Encourage learners to reflect on the tasks/processes that they carried out together during the project. The small images may help them remember some of the tasks.

2 Ask learners to discuss how they helped their group using the useful language provided.

Answers and formative assessment: Open. Look for learners' responses that demonstrate reflection on their individual contribution to the group's project at different stages.

Differentiation:

Give support by prompting learners with questions to remind them of any examples that you witnessed where they helped their group. Ask them to recall something they think they did well, and then to consider how that helped the group as a whole.

Give extra challenge by asking learners to develop their responses further. *I helped my group to … because I … One idea I had was …. This helped my group because ….*

What have I learned how to do?

Good for: Helping learners identify how their skills have developed further during the project.

Activity: With the learners, read Sofia's statement about what she has learned how to do. Following this model, learners reflect on their own skill development and write their response in the space provided.

Answers and formative assessment: Can learners reflect on a skill (as opposed to a fact) they have learned?

Differentiation:

Give support by creating and working through a model dialogue and questions similar to that provided in in downloadable 2.8 (section 2.6 'What have I learned how to do?'). Use this to clarify the difference between learning a fact and learning a new skill.

Give extra challenge by asking learners to develop their responses further. *Before the work project I did not know how to [named skill]. Now I can [named skill] because I [activity described].*

Plenary

Activity: Share some effective responses to the last activity with the whole class. If possible, explain briefly what they will be learning about in the next project that you will be working on and what the outcome of that project will be. Help them to break this process down. *What do you think we will need to do? What do you think we will need to find out? Who/what could help us?* Invite the learners to think about how what they have learned in this project (knowledge/skills/understanding) will help them to achieve the outcome for the next project.

Answers and formative assessment: Open. Look for answers that demonstrate appropriate reflection on how their skills can be applied in a different learning context. Can learners give responses (verbal/written) that successfully reflect on what they learned during the garden project with support? Can learners give responses (verbal/written) that successfully reflect how they helped their group?

Reflection: Refer learners to the learning goals in their books (I can talk about what I learned. I can say what I did with my group). See page xxiv for a suggested procedure.

Home learning ideas

Activity: Ask the learners to tell parents/care givers (and, if appropriate, extended family members) about their work project – what they have enjoyed and what they have learned.

Home–school link: Explain to parents/care givers that the work project has now come to an end. Encourage them to ask learners questions about the things that they have enjoyed and skills that they have learned.

Taking it further

In this project, learners have used their understanding from research to create a role play. A logical next step would be to capture some of this imagined experience in writing. Learners could write a range of appropriate non-fiction: non-chronological reports, simple recounts or instructions.

Talking about the world of work can also be an excellent way to bring in further expertise from the community your school serves. Parents, extended family members and school employees could again be potential sources. School employees who have prior experience in sectors outside education would bring a valuable comparative perspective to offer the learners. Adults with experience of doing the same job in different countries could help shape learners' global perspective on this issue.

Learners enjoy taking on adult roles in imaginative play. It is unfortunately the case that for many learners, taking on an adult role is their reality. World Day against Learner Labour is on 12 June. This would be an excellent opportunity to focus on the right to an education and to be free from exploitation, if it fits in with your school year. UNICEFs figures state that this issue directly impacts on the lives of nearly one in ten learners worldwide. Fifty percent do hazardous work that is harmful to their development. Learners can, of course, learn responsibility through performing tasks at home like tidying up after themselves. Explore the difference between work that is, and work that is not, appropriate for learners to do. Some suggested resources are available on UNICEF's website, on their Rights Respecting Schools toolkit.

Learners who have successfully completed this project will have developed a range of skills and attributes that would enable them to attempt the Cambridge International Primary Global Perspectives Challenges 'Working and having a job' and 'Working together' with enhanced confidence.

4 How can we save water?

Introduction

The structure of this project is similar to previous projects, but progression is provided by learners applying similar skills to a more challenging learning outcome. Progression can again be enhanced by reducing the extent of support through scaffolding and modelling, and moving learners to independent learning activities sooner.

To begin with, learners look at an image that shows different uses of water. Allow the discussion to build on elements of the learners' own understanding of the different uses of water shown. Make a note of any misconceptions that emerge so that these can be addressed in due course. Learners should now have a good level of experience of thinking about their own responses before opening up discussions in pairs/groups. Questions: *Who is using water? What are they using water for? Are they using water carefully?*

Next, learners examine different ways that people use water in school (Lesson 1: Analysis). They consider their prior understanding of how they use water based on their own experience. They consider what action is appropriate in the event that they find a tap that is leaking.

They conduct research that develops their ability to record data (Lesson 2: Research). The learners prepare questions, then ask other people about how and when they use water.

The learners consider evidence from a video to deepen their understanding of the importance of saving water (Lesson 3: Evaluation). They construct sentences that will help them express their own thoughts on this issue.

In the next lesson, learners use their knowledge and understanding about why it is important to save water, and they share their understanding of practical steps that they can take. (Lesson 4: Collaboration). They develop imaginative play to explore water-saving strategies. Following their role play, they explain which ideas for saving water they think are most interesting to them personally.

Learners build on their role play to tell other people about their understanding of what they can do to use water responsibly (Lesson 5: Communication). They work on their use of voice and gesture to present their ideas to an audience. Finally, they reflect on what they have learned about the importance of saving water (Lesson 6: Reflection). They are also asked to consider what new knowledge, skills and understanding they have developed with support. As with previous projects, learners consider what aspects of the project they have enjoyed.

Cross-curricular links and themes

This project lends itself particularly well to integration with theme-based learning on water, including understanding the central importance of fresh water to all life on Earth.

The theme of different kinds of employment developed throughout this project builds understanding relevant to UN Sustainable Development Goal 6 Ensuring clean water and sanitation is available to all. The UN marks World Water Day on 22 March.

Building understanding of the importance of clean water can be used to develop learners' understanding that they have the right to the best health care possible, clean water to drink, healthy food and a clean and safe environment to live in. All adults and children should have information about how to stay safe and healthy. This fits with UN Rights of the Child Article 24: Every child has the right to the best possible health. Governments must provide good quality health care, clean water, nutritious food, a clean environment and education on health and wellbeing so that children can stay healthy. Richer countries must help poorer countries achieve this.

Learners have opportunities to apply their knowledge and understanding of, and skills in:	
Reading skills	• Reading and listening to a range of water-themed books, drawing on background information and vocabulary provided • Making links from their reading to their own experiences of using water – including using it responsibly • Demonstrating their understanding of explicit meaning in text provided about how water can be used responsibly
Writing skills	• Selecting and developing content appropriate to conveying a 'saving water' message to a specified audience in school
Speaking and listening skills	• Listening to others (learners and adults) and responding appropriately • Asking and listening carefully to questions • Listening to and giving instructions • Engaging in imaginative play, enacting work roles and situations • Speaking clearly to an audience • Showing awareness of the listener through non-verbal communication
Scientific skills	• Applying their knowledge that plants need water to grow • Applying their knowledge of the need for a healthy diet, including the right types of food and water

Before beginning work on this project, it would be helpful if learners have knowledge of or have had previous experience of:
• Speaking to a group to share an experience • Answering questions and explaining further when asked • Understanding that people speak in different ways for different purposes and meaning • Understanding that texts for different purposes look different – for example, use of photographs, diagrams • Recognising different parts of a book – for example, title page, contents and understanding their functions • Engaging in imaginative play, enacting simple characters or situations • Using simple fieldwork and observational skills to study the physical layout of their school • Looking at a vertical aerial photograph showing the features and layout of their school from a 'bird's eye' view 'directly' above (or familiarity with other simple maps or plans) • Using abstract symbols used on maps representing the features of an area, and the use of a key to identify what is shown • Answering questions by sorting and organising data or objects in a variety of ways – for example, using block graphs and pictograms with practical resources – and discussing the results. • Understanding that plants need light and water to grow • Understanding that people need access to a healthy diet, including the right types of food and water.

Assessment focus
The focus skills for this project is Analysis. The following downloadables will support you with assessing learners' attainment against the curriculum framework: • Downloadable 4.7 (Assessment guidance sheet: Analysis) • Downloadable 4.8 (Assessment record sheet: Analysis)
For a general introduction to the approach to assessment in this course, see page xxiii

Getting started

Good for: Activating learners' prior understanding of the use of water, and different people's perspectives on what they use it for.

Activity:

1 Display the picture and ask learners what they can see a lot of people using (water). Ask the learners to spot the four characters – Zara, Sofia, Arun and Marcus. What are the characters doing? What would it be like if they did not have any clean fresh water to use?

Ask questions about the different elements of the picture. For example, *What is Arun doing? What can we see in his picture? Where do fish live? What are Sofia and Marcus doing? What is Zara doing? Why is it important for us to wash our hands?* Draw attention to the place for water bottles to be stored. *Why is it important for us to drink water? What would we feel like if we weren't able to drink?*

Draw attention to the small watering can next to the plants. *What is this for?* Draw attention to the reading area, which contains a display of water-themed books. Read the titles together. What do the learners think that they could read about in these books? Show them the globe. What do they think this is? Why is it that we can see so much blue? Finally, establish that the books, posters and pictures all show water.

Answers: This will depend on the learners' prior experience and their interests. Use the discussion of the image to gain understanding of what interests them.

Differentiation:

Give support by showing images of water use in a familiar context before looking at the image in the book, or showing them aspects of your own classroom that are similar to the image shown in respect of how water is supplied/used. Ask them to describe their experience of using water.

Give extra challenge by providing images of water use taken in contrasting locations. For example, if your location is characterised by heavy rainfall, show them images of a location with low rainfall – or vice versa. (Māwsynrām in India is an area with heavy rainfall. Farafra in Egypt is in a very arid environment. Images from Google Earth could be used to stimulate discussion of how it would feel to be in a very wet or in a very dry place).

Is the way that learners can see water being used in these images similar or different to what they might see locally? *Why might water be used in a different way in different places? What different kinds of activities need water?*

Provide images of rainfall and ask learners to describe their personal experience of rain, or what they know about rain from other sources – for example, information books, stories and other media. Point out the classroom display board that features the water cycle. Ask *What do they think that the display is showing?*

4.1 How do we use water at school?

LEARNING OBJECTIVES: ANALYSIS

1A.01 Identifying perspectives: Say something known about an issue

1A.02 Interpreting data: Talk about information recorded in pictograms or graphic organisers

1A.03 Making connections: Talk about simple, personal consequences of own actions

1A.04 Solving problems: Choose a possible solution to an issue from a range of actions given

LEARNING GOALS

- I can talk about where we use water at school
- I can talk about what happens when I do things

LEARNING ATTRIBUTES

This lesson gives learners the opportunity to be:

- Confident in working with information and ideas – their own and those of others

Resources needed

Learner's Skills Book pages 82–86

Images of objects appropriate for the Starter Activity (see below)

Appropriately simplified base map of the school for the learners to mark on the location of taps (see details below)

Optional: Old taps that can be dismantled so that the learners can see where water flows, clipboards, coloured pencils (optional)

Starter

Good for: Formative assessment of learners' understanding of the uses of water. Learners who consistently point appropriately may well need further challenge. Learners who consistently point incorrectly may well need additional support.

Activity: Tell the learners that, in this project, we will be finding out how we use water. Today, we are thinking of all of the different ways in which we use water at school. Show an image – for example, an indoor plant in school. Ask: *Does this plant need water? Point to the window if you think Yes. Point to the door if you think No. Point to the ceiling if you think Maybe*. Repeat with a range of images that the learners might be familiar with, which do or do not need water (e.g. some kind of animal or bird, some kind of insect, some kind of inanimate object). Then move on to actions – for example, *cleaning your teeth, brushing your hair*. Choose some where the need for water is not immediately apparent – for example, *eating fruit*. Establish that water is needed: to grow the fruit in the first place, to wash it, to wash our hands before we eat, and so on.

Where do we use water in school?

Good for: Learners to gain confidence in talking about information represented using images. Formative assessment of the learners' level of prior understanding.

Activity:

1 Ask learners to work with a partner. They should look carefully at the map of the school and discuss the questions together. Take feedback and discuss as a class.

2 If possible, provide the learners with the opportunity to go around your school (or into certain rooms) in appropriately supervised groups to note the location of taps. You will need to prepare and hand out copies of a simple plan of your school layout, or of the parts of the school you would like them to visit. Ideally, learners should be working with a partner with one copy of the base map between two. They will need a clipboard and pen/pencil (or an appropriate digital equivalent). Notice the taps as you go around the school. Establish what they are used for in each place.

Explain that when they find a tap, they should draw the tap symbol (copied from the key in the book) at the appropriate place on their copy of the plan. Show them how to look to see whether the tap is dripping, in which case they should draw a drip under their picture of a tap. (Note: if the tap is simply running because somebody has forgotten to turn it off, they should turn it off!) Alternatively, you could have one learner (supervised) investigate the taps in each room and report back, drawing the taps on a single map displayed for the whole class. If you are unable to provide a school map, you could simply write a list of rooms and have learners draw the tap symbol next to the name of the room.

If possible, arrange for the learners to be shown the main 'stop cock' or valve where water enters the school.

Suggested answers:

1 a Girls' toilets and boys' toilets.
  b Class 1, 2 and 3.
  c The office.
  d Girls' toilets, boys' toilets and Class 3.

2 Open. Look for answers that accurately reflect your context.

Can learners locate taps and draw symbols appropriately – do they draw the correct number of taps in each room? Can they differentiate between taps that drip and taps that do not? Can they record the location and number of dripping and non-dripping taps appropriately on their base maps?

Differentiation:

Give support by helping learners who have limited experience of using a map. You could show them a satellite image of their school using an application such as Google Earth. Spend some time locating familiar features. Show them a map of the local area that corresponds to the satellite image. Draw attention to the key. Establish that maps have symbols on them to show us important features of the area.

Scaffold a discussion based on the first question. For example, *Which room has four taps? Let's see? Can it be the office? No, it can't be the office because I can't see any taps at all.*

Give extra challenge by asking learners to create their own base map of the school (rather than use one supplied by you) and then having them mark the location of taps in the same way.

Collect water that comes out of a dripping tap in a given period of time – for example, one minute. Ask them to imagine how much water would be lost over the course of an hour, a day and so on. This could be expressed in terms of non-standard units with which the learners are familiar – for example, a water bottle, a sink full or anything else you or they could think of.

What is the best thing to do?

Good for: Learners to think and talk about the consequences of their actions.

Activity:

1 Read through Zara's three possible courses of action with the learners, checking understanding (including of the term 'member of staff': any adult who works there). Allow learners to explore and discuss what to do in pairs, then feed back as a class.

2 As a class, discuss what learners would do if they found a dripping tap. (The 'best' thing to do might depend on the context – for example, at school, at home, in a public place). Learners record their answer in their book. Reinforce your school guidance on when it is and is not appropriate to talk to an adult when discussing what the best thing to do in a public place is.

Answers and formative assessment: Look for answers that demonstrate understanding appropriately. 1: If Zara put the plug in, the sink would fill up. Eventually the water would overflow and go all over the floor. 2: If she left the plug out, the water would continue to flow down the plug. A lot of water would be wasted. 3: If she told a member of staff, they would arrange for the tap to be repaired. It would not drip any more.

Look for answers that identify positive consequences of learners drawing attention to this problem.

Differentiation:

Give support by conducting this discussion in a small group and looking at a real sink.

Give extra challenge by asking learners to discuss their understanding further. Where do they think the water in the tap comes from? What happens to it after it goes down the plughole or the overflow pipe?

Why do we use water in school?

Good for: Building understanding of the variety of reasons why water is used in school. (Later in the project, you can use this to help identify ways in which water can be used sensibly). Also, reinforcing the idea that our actions have consequences.

Activity:

1 Explain to the learners that Arun and Sofia have been thinking about why they use water in school. Read the characters' answers to the questionnaire, checking learners' understanding. 'Why did Arun

need water?' He had noticed that the plant was dry. 'What happened?' He gave the plant some water and after a week the plant had recovered. 'Why did Sofia need water?' She had been running and she was thirsty. 'What happened?' She drank water and wasn't thirsty any more so she could run again.

Give the learners time to reflect on an occasion that they needed to use water in school. Why was this? What happened? If learners are short of ideas, you could prompt them with clues to activities such as washing their hands after a messy activity, dipping paintbrushes into water while painting, cleaning up a minor injury after playtime, doing a science activity, filling up the bird bowl in the school garden, flushing the toilet (if you feel it appropriate). Take some whole-class feedback and make some notes on the board or flipchart–grouping learners' responses under appropriate headings such as 'Staying healthy', 'Keeping clean', and so on. Add these notes to your working wall' (see page xxiv for explanation).

2 Ask learners to record their own written answer in the book, following the model set by Arun and Sofia.

Answers: Open. Look for clear explanation of cause and consequence.

Differentiation:

Give support by providing images of activities that the learners have taken part in where water was used – for example, painting – to aid discussion. These could be either photos taken by you, or alternatively other suitable images that you have found online.

Give extra challenge by asking learners to develop their answers. What would happen if water was not available?

Plenary

Activity: Display the questions explored during the course of this lesson: 'Where do we use water in school?' and 'Why do we use water in school?' Give the learners time for think–pair–share and invite some responses. Note some appropriate responses. Explain that next time we will be focusing on two questions: 'How do other people use water?' and 'How can we find out more?' What are the learners' thoughts on these questions at this point? Ask the learners to consider different ways that they have found out information in previous projects. Would any of these strategies work?

Answers: Open.

Reflection: Refer learners to the learning goals in their books (I can talk about where we use water at school. I can talk about what happens when I do things). See page xxiv for a suggested procedure.

Home learning ideas

Activity: Ask learners to make a map of their home and mark on it where they can see water (i.e. taps, showers, toilets). Ask them to devise a key for features other than taps. Put these maps on display and use them to discuss water use later in the project and to help identify ways in which water can be used with (greater) care.

Home–school link: Explain to parents/care givers that the children are starting a project about the importance of water and the need to look after it. Say that it would be helpful for their children's project if the children could make a map of their home showing the location of water – for example, taps, showers and so on.

4.2 How do other people use water?

LEARNING OBJECTIVES: RESEARCH

1Rs.03 Conducting research: Begin to participate in simple investigations and ask basic questions to find information and opinions

1Rs.04 Recording findings: Record information on a given issue in pictograms or simple graphic organisers

LEARNING GOALS

- I can find out about how people use water
- I can record information in a chart

LEARNING ATTRIBUTES

This lesson gives learners the opportunity to be:

- Responsible for themselves, responsive to and respectful of others

Resources needed

Learner's Skills Book pages 86–91

Downloadable 4.1 (two charts for learners to record results)

Audio 11 with transcript of how different people use water

Starter

Good for: Activating learners' prior understanding of handling data.

Activity: Recap the previous lesson by asking learners to name some activities they do in school that involve water. Say that you want to find out how often the class uses water during the day for two of those activities: hand washing and having a drink. Ask for ideas as to how you could do this. Each learner could simply *count* the number of times they did these things, but would they remember at the end of the school day? If someone suggests *recording* each time a learner washes their hands or has a drink, ask *how* they would do this.

Prompt (if no-one suggests it): could they make a chart? How would each learner mark the chart **a** for drinking and **b** for hand washing: can they suggest a simple symbol to use (e.g. a picture of a hand)? Would it be useful to divide the school day up in some way on the chart? How would they suggest dividing it (e.g. into morning and afternoon, before and after break, or by hour)? Either draw a large basic chart to the learners' specification, or use a simple blank chart that you have pre-prepared, adding in the headings that the learners suggest. It might look like this:

Morning	Lunch time	Afternoon

Add a key to draw symbols to represent handwashing or drinking water.

Alternatively, divide up the day into periods of time that reflect your class's routine (e.g. register time, before break, morning break, story time, etc).

Ask learners to fill in this chart over the course of the day. When the learners have completed the data recording for a day, use the chart to ask questions. Again, appropriate questions to ask will reflect the learners' prior understanding of handling data in this way – for example, *How many learners took a drink of water between 9 o' clock and 10 o'clock?* Or *What was the time when most learners washed their hands?*

Differentiation:

Give support by providing a pre-populated chart and asking some closed questions to start off with – for example, *True or false: five learners washed their hands at lunchtime?'*

Give extra challenge by asking learners to use the chart to devise their own questions and to share these with a partner.

How can we talk to people about using water?

Good for: Considering different people's perspectives about why water is important.

Activity:

1 Explain to the learners that they are going to hear three different people talk about a reason that water is important to them. These people are the school cook, Arun's friend and Sofia's neighbour. Draw attention to the photos. Ask learners to discuss in pairs why they think each person might use water. Explain that there are some clues in the photos.

2 Play Audio 11, noting when different characters speak if needed. Listen to the audio and check answers. Learners complete the sentences in the Learner's Skills Book.

Talk about other people who use water as part of their job. If you have completed the workplace project prior to this unit, you may well have discussed professions such as firefighters or medical staff, and learners may be able to suggest how those people might use water in their jobs.

Answers:

2 a The school cook uses water to *cook rice/food* and to *wash/clean tools/pans/things in the kitchen.*

b Arun's friend uses water to *fill the rabbit's water bottle.*

c Sofia's neighbour uses water to *water the flowers and vegetables.*

Differentiation:

Give support by asking learners if they know people who use water in similar ways to those described by the characters.

Give extra challenge by asking learners how they could make a chart that they could use to record the named person's (such as the school cook or Arun's friend) use of water for the given purpose.

How can we find out more?

Good for: Helping learners understand how to collect information on a given issue and record their findings in pictograms or simple graphic organisers

Activity:

1 Explain that Sofia wanted to find out more about when her neighbour used water on his garden. Show the learners her chart. *What did Sofia find out?* What question do the learners think that Sofia asked her neighbour?

2 Explain that Arun also found out more about when her friend used water for her pet rabbit. What can they learn from the chart? What question do they think Arun asked?

Answers and formative assessment:

1 From the first chart, we can find out when Sofia's neighbour waters her plants. He waters his plants in the morning and in the evening.

2 From the second chart, we can find out when Arun's friend topped up the rabbit's water bottle over the course of a week. She topped up the bottle a total of 12 times: once on Monday, twice on Tuesday, once on Wednesday, twice on Thursday, once on Friday, twice on Saturday and three times on Sunday.

Differentiation:

Give support by asking closed questions such as *Did Sofia's neighbour water the plants in the morning?* (Yes) *Did she water them at midday?* (No). If learners still find it challenging to use Arun's chart, ask similar closed questions appropriate to the data shown here. *Did Arun's friend fill her rabbit's water bottle every day?* (Yes) *How do we know?* (At least one bottle is shown for each day in the chart).

Give extra challenge by asking the learners to suggest possible reasons for the pattern of water use shown in the tables – for example, *it is a good idea to avoid the heat of the day when watering plants. The rabbit might have been more thirsty on Sunday because it was a hot day, or maybe Arun's friend had more time to let the rabbit run free and it became thirsty as a result.*

How can we show people what we found out?

Good for: Developing learners' understanding of ways in which data can show information about an issue.

Activity:

1 Discuss with the learners the different ways that they use water in their family. They should look at the list provided and add any other uses not in the list. Give them time to record their own family's uses of water by ticking the boxes.

2 Explain to the learners that they are going to talk about water use to somebody in their family. They will find out how often that person uses water for a particular reason, like Arun and Sofia did. First,

they should choose one of the uses of water from the list in 1, and put a circle around it. They should also record who they will talk to about their use of water and what question they will ask.

3 Talk to the learners about the different ways that Arun and Sofia organised their information in their charts. Talk about how each of them drew a picture to represent information – Sofia drew a watering can to show when her neighbour watered the garden and Arun drew a picture of a water bottle to represent each time that her friend topped up his rabbit's drinking bottle.

   Ask the learners to consider which kind of chart would be best for recording the information that they would like to collect, and to think of an appropriate simple picture they could draw. (Remind them that they will have to copy it several times!)

4 Give out copies of downloadable 4.1 so that learners can record their own information.

Answers and formative assessment: Open. Check that they choose a chart that is appropriate to the use of water that they have identified. If they want to record something that happens over the course of a day, then a chart showing the times of the day is more appropriate.

If they want to record something that happens over the course of a week, then a chart showing days of the week is more appropriate. Check that their question is appropriate to the use of water that they have identified. Prompt the learners to check also as far as possible that the person that they have identified will be able to answer the question they will ask them.

Differentiation:

Give support by providing a number of possible symbols that learners could draw to record their information – some of which would be appropriate for the uses of water that the learners describe and some of them less appropriate. Which would be good to use to record their information? Why? If you anticipate that some learners might find it challenging to complete this activity with somebody at home, liaise with colleagues in school who might be available to help by answering the learners' questions.

Give extra challenge by asking learners to devise further questions about the use of water. Challenge them to suggest ways in which they could measure and record how *much* water is used.

Plenary

Activity: Ask learners to predict what they think the results of their research might be. When the research has been completed, compare the results with these predictions. Display some examples of the learners' tables when the research has been completed. Point out various tables and ask the class what they think that the learner was trying to find out. Can learners see any patterns in their results? How could they explain them?

Answers and formative assessment: Open. This will depend on the learners' ideas and preferences. Look for responses that show good use of reasoning skills.

Reflection: Refer learners to the learning goals in their books (I can find out about how people use water. I can record information in a chart). See page xxiv for a suggested procedure.

Home learning ideas

Activity: Give learners the chance to make a copy of their chart to use with their family at home. They could use it to find out how/when/where the members of their family use water. They could then bring the chart back to school with their findings.

Home–school link: Explain that the children have been learning how to conduct a simple survey about water use. Ask parents/care givers if they could help their children to do a simple survey with a few family members or neighbours.

4.3 What do I think about saving water?

LEARNING OBJECTIVES: EVALUATION

1E.02 Evaluating perspectives and arguments: State an opinion about a given issue

ADDITIONAL LEARNING OBJECTIVES

1Rs.02 Information skills: Talk about information on a given issue in sources provided

LEARNING GOALS

- I can say what I think about saving water

LEARNING ATTRIBUTES

This lesson gives learners the opportunity to be:

- Engaged intellectually and socially, ready to make a difference

Resources needed

Learner's Skills Book pages 92–94

Video 4

Either Downloadable 4.2 ('Fact or opinion?') or an image of someone using water in a local context that is familiar to the learners. The image should be capable of being enlarged/projected for a whole-class discussion

A series of statements about the image: some purely factual, some giving opinions

Starter

Good for: Reactivating learners' prior understanding of opinion.

Activity: Show an image of a person using water in a local context that is familiar to the learners. Have a series of statements written on cards. (Alternatively, display the images on downloadable 4.2 or distribute copies). Some statements should be purely factual – for example, *The person is using a …* Some should give opinions. Make sure that the opinions contain a range that includes subjective feelings (e.g., *It would be fun to* …) and value judgements (e.g. *That is a clever way to* …). If you are using the downloadable, it provides a fact and an opinion related to each photo.

Say that you want to sort the cards into facts and opinions but you need the learners' help. Hold each statement up in turn and read it together. Ask the learners *Is this a fact or an opinion?* Ask the learners to point to the window (or similar) if they think that the statement is a fact. Ask them to point to the door (or similar) if they think that the statement is an opinion. After they have pointed, choose learners to explain their reasons for pointing one way or the other.

Answers and formative assessment: Place the correctly sorted cards on prominent display appropriately underneath the two headings 'Facts' and 'Opinions'. Use this discussion to find out any misconceptions at this stage and address them.

What can we find out about saving water?

Good for: Building learners' understanding of how to say what they think in response to someone else's opinion.

Activity:

1 Read Arun's speech bubble with the learners. Take some initial suggestions and make some notes of these on your board. There may be some misconceptions. It is not necessary to correct these until after learners have seen the video.

2 Show learners the video. Allow the learners to answer the questions. Check answers. 

3 Repeat the video. Pause on an image that depicts flooding and allow some further time for think–pair–share to consider Arun's question. Establish that it is indeed the case that some people suffer as a result of flooding. This does not mean that fresh clean water is not precious – flood water is not clean.

In some places, water is very scarce. Pause on an image of drinking clean water and drought to aid further discussion and clarification. If you feel it is relevant to your setting, you may also wish to mention the process of desalination in reference to sea water not being good to drink. It is certainly the case that sea water can be made into drinkable water, and this is common in certain parts of the world. (This does, however, require the use of a lot of energy).

Learners answer the questions with a partner.

Revisit the learners' initial thoughts that you noted. How have their opinions changed in the light of the information they have learned from watching the video? Use the Did You Know? box, if you wish, to lead into a discussion about what causes it to rain (and about the water cycle).

Answers and formative assessment:

2 a Yes; b No; c Yes.

3 a (Example) There will not be enough water for everyone who needs it.

b (Example) Turn off the shower when you have finished; turn off the tap when you brush your teeth; collect rain water for the plants; find out the best ways to save water where you live.

Can the learners suggest an appropriate response for Arun to tell his friend? Can they demonstrate understanding that the first part of the statement (that some places have too much water) is reasonable, but the second part (we don't need to save it) does not follow?

Differentiation:

Give support by scaffolding the process of responding to an opinion further. Provide sentence starters such as *It is true that … It is not true that …*

Give extra challenge by asking learners to explain the different opinions. For example, *Why might [name] think that was true? What might cause there to be 'too much' water? What would that feel like? Why is it still important to look after fresh clean water? How could Arun persuade [name]?*

Why should we save water?

Good for: Constructing statements relevant to a given issue

Activity: Learners complete the matching task.

Suggested answers:

1 a People, animals and plants need water to help them grow and stay healthy.

b There is a lot of water in the world but it is not all clean.

c The water in the oceans is too salty to drink.

d There are a lot of people in the world and they all need clean water.

Differentiation:

Give support by providing the sentence beginnings and endings as two separate sets of cards. Learners work with support to match them up taking the cards one at a time and checking if they make sense when matched.

Give extra challenge by asking learners in pairs to formulate their own sentences about why it is important to save water. They can write these on strips of paper. They can then cut these up and challenge other pairs to reassemble the sentences correctly.

How can I say what I think about saving water?

Good for: Selecting information learned from a source (in this case, a video) in order to express and justify an opinion.

Activity: Read the model opinions provided by Zara and Marcus. Additionally/alternatively, provide the learners with a statement of opinion linked to an issue in your locality. Ask learners to construct their own statement of opinion using the sentence starter provided. Ask them to reread their sentence to check that they have really explained why saving water is important, and to add a second sentence if necessary. For example, if they wrote *I think we should save water because it is important*, can they now give a *reason* why it is important?

Answers and formative assessment: Open. Look for responses that provide a reasoned explanation. For example, *We should save water because it is important. I would not like it if we could not drink/swim/wash. We should save water because everybody needs clean water to live/stay healthy/stay clean*, and so on.

Differentiation:

Give support by providing additional worked examples and discussing them. For example, *We should save water because it can be fun to play in. I would like to save washing-up water to clean my bike.*

Give extra challenge by providing counter-arguments to the statements that the learners have constructed. Stress that these are not your real opinion – but some people could think like this. How could they persuade a person who thinks in this way that saving water is important?

Plenary

Activity: Share some of the opinions that learners wrote down about why we should save water. Ask the learners how they could explain to younger learners (e.g. in pre-school or kindergarten) why they should be careful to save water. Take some suggestions about how they could present the information they have learned for a younger audience so that they could understand. Then share another water-saving idea with the learners (e.g. reusing shower water by watering the flowers with it) and ask for their help. Ask *How could we explain this with words and actions?* Give time for think–pair–share.

Answers and formative assessment: Open. Look for appropriate ideas and justifications – especially those that are based on the learners' understanding of the audience. Learners may find it appropriate to perform their suggestions.

Reflection: Refer learners to the learning goals in their book (I can say what I think about saving water). See page xxiv for a suggested procedure.

4.4 What different ways are there to save water?

LEARNING OBJECTIVES: COLLABORATION

1Cl.01 Working together: Work positively with others, sharing resources while working independently or with others

ADDITIONAL LEARNING OBJECTIVES

1Cm.01 Communicating information: Answer questions with relevant information about a given issue

1Cm.02 Listening and responding: Listen to others in class discussions and respond with simple questions

LEARNING GOALS

- I can work with my group to ask and answer questions about saving water

LEARNING ATTRIBUTES

This lesson gives learners the opportunity to be:

- Innovative and equipped for new and future challenges

Resources needed

Learner's Skills Book pages 95–98

Downloadable 4.3 (pictures to support water-saving ideas)

Images/slogans from a water-saving campaign run locally (if available)

Items that are appropriate for demonstrating the careful use of water – for example, *a shower head, a bucket, a watering can, a washing-up bowl, plastic taps and so on* (or downloadable 4.3)

Starter

Good for: Preparing learners to choose a possible solution to an issue from a range of actions given.

Activity: Show the learners one of the items that is used in connection with water (see Resources needed). (Alternatively, display the images on downloadable 4.3, one by one). Say that you would like to think of ways to use water more carefully. Can the learners think of a way of using the item to help waste less water? Establish ways in which they could. Repeat with the other items.

How can we save water?

Good for: Introducing learners to the idea that there are different ways of performing the same action – some of which use more resources than others.

Activity:

1–2 Explain to the learners that, now they know it is important to save water, they are going to be thinking about ways to use less water. They will then use their best ideas to tell other people how to use water carefully.

Learners look at the pairs of photos and answer the questions.

Read the information in the Did You Know? box with the learners. How could they find out how much water they use if they *don't* turn the tap off while they are brushing their teeth? Do they have any suggestions? Would they like to try this at home?

Suggested answers:

1 **a** tomatoes; **b** [washing in a bowl].

2 **a** cars; **b** [washing with a hose]; **c** [washing from a bucket].

Are the learners able to explain the difference between the two ways of washing **a** tomatoes and **b** a car, and why one way wastes more water than the other way?

Differentiation:

Give support by demonstrating (or if possible, giving learners the opportunity to try for themselves) practically that washing an item in a small bowl uses less water than washing it under a running tap, by collecting the water used. Discuss how this process is shown in the photographs.

Give extra challenge by asking learners to think of other things that we do that use water. What ways of performing the same action might use less (or more) water?

How can pictures show people how to save water?

Good for: Developing understanding of further different ways to save water.

Activity:

1 Explain that pictures can tell us what the right thing to do is. Point out any examples in your classroom or mention any others that learners in your setting are likely to be familiar with (e.g. an emergency exit sign). Why might a picture sometimes be better than writing for showing what you need to do?

(Answers might include: it shows the message more quickly, it is good for people who cannot read, you are more likely to notice it).

Draw attention to Image 1 in the book. Discuss as a class what the picture might mean. Once learners have understood what the picture is telling us, ask why the picture is telling us to have a shower for only five minutes (i.e. to save water).

Ask learners to talk about Images 2 and 3 with a partner and to write down what they think each image is telling us. Compare answers as a class.

2 Ask learners if they can think of any more ideas for saving water (either for themselves at home, or for other people who use water – for example, in their jobs). Take a few suggestions. Then ask learners to think of a way of drawing a picture that shows an idea for saving water, in a similar way to the images they have just been looking at.

Suggested answers and formative assessment:

1 **a** Have a shower for only five minutes.

b Collect water in a bucket when it rains. Use the water to water the plants when it is sunny.

c Do not leave the tap on when you are brushing your teeth.

Check that learners' answers convey understanding that the images are telling us ways to use water carefully.

Differentiation:

Give support by breaking down the drawing task into smaller steps. Ask the learners to suggest actions that they do that use water. Ask them to suggest a way of doing the task that would use a lot of water. Then ask them to suggest a way a way of doing the task that would use less water. If they wanted to make a picture to show this, what could they draw?

Give extra challenge by asking the learners to suggest further everyday tasks that could be done using collected rainwater.

How can we talk about saving water in our group?

Good for: Looking at and assessing various ways of saving water; working cooperatively within a group to share information and make a decision together.

Activity:

1 Remind learners about your expectations of appropriate learning behaviour in group work. Take some suggestions about good ways to work together (e.g. listening to others, taking turns). Explain to the learners that they are going to work with other learners to share their ideas about how to use water carefully using the picture they have drawn.

Put learners into groups. Draw attention to and explain the simple flowchart that shows how they will be working. Allow time for each learner to show and explain their picture, explaining how their idea works and how it will save water, and for the other group members to ask them questions. Swap roles until all the learners have shown their picture and have both asked and answered questions

2 Tell learners to agree, as a group, which is the best idea for using water carefully. They write notes in their book to explain what the idea is and why they think it is a good idea.

Answers and formative assessment: Open. Look for examples of learners explaining clearly how the actions they drew in their picture will help to save water.

Differentiation:

Give support by modelling and scaffolding some appropriate responses to the images.

Give extra challenge by asking learners to identify possible challenges. Why might some people find it hard to use water carefully in this way? For example, *What might people do if they don't understand that the supply of water is limited? How could we help them to understand better?*

Plenary

Activity: Put the learners' drawings on display and ask learners to reflect on **a** what they have learned about different ways to save water, and **b** how they worked together as a group. Ask: *What did you learn from listening to the other learners in your group? Did you work together well? How did you help each other to learn?*

Answers and formative assessment: Open. Look for answers where learners identify how other learners' perspectives enriched their own understanding. For example, *Jamila's uncle collects water like this. He never has to turn on the tap to water the vegetables.* Look for answers that suggest the learners understand how to work collaboratively and can recognise whether or not they achieved it.

Reflection: Refer learners to the learning goals in their books (I can work with my group to ask and answer questions about saving water). See page xxiv for a suggested procedure.

Home learning ideas

Activity: Learners could set themselves a practical task that involves saving water at home (and maybe ask someone to take a photo of it to bring in). Alternatively, they could draw a picture of themselves using water carefully and write about their experience.

Home–school link: Ask parents to talk about ideas for responsible water use with their children and to help them record a water-saving action that the children tried out – for example, by encouraging them to make a drawing of it.

4.5 How can we tell other people how to use water carefully?

LEARNING OBJECTIVES: COMMUNICATION

1Cm.01 Communicating information: Answer questions with relevant information about a given issue

1Cm.02 Listening and responding: Listen to others in class discussions and respond with simple questions

LEARNING GOALS

- I can tell other people about using water carefully

LEARNING ATTRIBUTES

This lesson gives learners the opportunity to be:

- Engaged intellectually and socially, ready to make a difference

Resources needed

Learner's Skills Book pages 99–103

Downloadable 4.4 ('What shall we do in our show and tell?' – planning table)

Downloadable 4.5 ('What shall we do in our show and tell?' – Worked Example)

Audio 12 with transcript of how characters save water, and Audio 13 with words for the chant

Items that the learners have identified that they will need for demonstrating the careful use of water (see the planning sheet downloadable 4.4) – for example, *watering cans, washing-up bowls, donated items* (e.g. plastic taps or shower heads) that it would be safe for learners to work with

Starter

Good for: Activating learners' understanding of the best way to communicate information.

Activity: Choose something that you do on a regular basis with the class. For example, many teachers spend time at the start of the day updating a chart that shows the day, date, weather conditions, timetable and so on. Explain that you are going to do this part of their routine in three different ways. You want them to decide which way is the clearest and easiest for them to understand.

For example, 1 Say what you are doing in a quiet, mumbling voice, not looking at the learners at all; 2 (The 'correct' way) Talk clearly and expressively, making eye contact with the learners, saying what you are going to do as you do it and using clear actions; 3 Do it very quickly and without saying much about what you are doing). Ask them to show what they think: *Put your hands up if you thought the first way was the clearest … the second way … the third way …?* Why was that? Give time for think–pair–share.

Answers and formative assessment: Open. Look for answers that describe elements of clear communication appropriately.

Differentiation:

Give support by exaggerating the poor features of the first and third deliveries.

Give extra challenge by asking learners to show you how they would deliver this particular communication in as clear a way as possible.

How could we do a show and tell?

Good for: Understanding what is involved in speaking to an audience on a given issue.

Activity:

1 Explain to the learners that they are going to be doing a 'show and tell' about how to use water carefully, using all the ideas they have learned in the project. To get some ideas about how to do this, you will start by finding out about the show and tell that Sofia, Arun, Marcus and Zara did.

Focus attention on the picture of Sofia, Arun, Marcus and Zara's presentation. Have them answer the questions in pairs, then conduct feedback as a class. Ask learners to speculate on what the learners might be saying.

2 Tell learners they are now going to listen to what the learners are saying in the picture. Play Audio 12. Revisit the predictions the learners made. Replay the audio. Have learners answer the question in the book by ticking the correct option.

3 Ask the learners to think of what questions they would ask the characters if they could meet with them. What would they like to find out?

4 Explain that Sofia, Arun, Marcus and Zara wanted their audience to remember really well what they have told them about saving water. So they decided to finish by reciting a chant that they made up. Play Audio 13. Alternatively, the words can be sung to the tune of 'I hear thunder.' Ask learners to listen to the chant or song the first time around, and then to join in the second time.

   If you wish, learners could make up an appropriate chant or song as a conclusion to their own show and tell too.

Answers and formative assessment:

1 **a** a tap, some carrots, a washing-up bowl, a watering can; **b** so that they can show the audience their idea for saving water; **c** that it is important to save water, and how to save water.

2 The second option is correct (Use the same water for washing vegetables and watering plants).

   Can the learners show understanding about the reason why the learners are holding the objects? Can they explain the purpose of the show and tell?

Differentiation:

Give support by providing sentence starters along the following lines: 'Arun, Sofia, Marcus and Zara want people to …' Arun, Sofia, Marcus and Zara don't want people to …'

Give extra challenge by asking learners to explain how the items that the characters are showing demonstrate each step in the process of saving and reusing water. *What happens first? Then what happens? Why?* and so on. Perform 'in role' as one of the group and respond to the questions the learners ask you. Prompt them to follow up on what you say with additional questions.

What shall we do in our show and tell?

Good for: Preparing to give a presentation.

Activity:

1 Make sure that learners are familiar with the meaning and concept of audience: the person/people who will be watching and listening. Talk about who the audience will be for the learners' own show and tell.

2 Put learners in groups. In their groups, they should decide on one reason why people use water and then think of a way that people could use water for that reason more carefully. Refer them back to Arun, Sofia, Marcus and Zara's example if necessary.

   They should think about what props they could use that will help their audience understand what they are explaining. Encourage them to draw a picture, either of the items or of a learner/learners using the items to demonstrate their water-saving idea.

3 Tell learners to start planning how they will work as a group to explain their idea. They should write each person's name, and then write and/or draw what that person will say. You can display downloadable 4.5 to show learners a model of how to do this. If you wish, give out downloadable 4.4 for their plan. Draw attention to the useful phrases provided in the box.

Answers and formative assessment: Learners' own answers: Learners will develop their own scripts, which might resemble the following:

Learner 1 We need water to brush our teeth. Some people waste water when they brush their teeth.

Learner 2 They leave the tap on and the water goes down the plug.

Learner 3 You do not have to waste the water. You can turn the tap off.

Learner 4 You can put some water on your brush. You can turn the tap off when you are done.

Differentiation:

Give support by going through the process of planning the presentation step by step. *How do people use water? How could people be more careful when they use water for this reason? What causes fresh water to be wasted? How could we stop this from happening?* Appropriate images taken locally would be useful for stimulating discussion.

Give extra challenge by asking learners to make up questions to find out more about the other groups' water-saving message.

What will our audience see and hear?

Good for: Learners to prepare a presentation that is clear and engaging.

Activity:

1 Remind learners that they will be talking to an audience, and it is very important that their audience can hear and see them well. Direct them to the list of tips. Can they add one more?

2 Get learners to practise saying the line 'It's easy to save water', following the advice on the 'Tips for speaking to an audience' sign. Ask them to listen to each other and give feedback.

3 Learners practise performing any actions that they will need to do in their show and tell, using the props they have chosen. Again, they should watch each other. Encourage helpful feedback about how they could demonstrate their actions more clearly.

Answers and formative assessment: Open. Look for appropriate use of voice and gesture. Can learners modify their voices so that what they say is clear and expressive? Can they perform actions so that what they are doing is clear to an audience?

Differentiation:

Give support by modelling some appropriate and clear ways of speaking their lines and showing the learners some clear gestures. Speak to the learners using your voice less effectively. Use some gestures that are less clear. Ask them which version was easier to understand and why. Encourage them to use the techniques they have identified as successful in their own performances.

Give extra challenge by asking learners to consider the needs of their target audience more precisely. Who are they going to be talking to? How can we make our message clear to them?

Plenary

Activity: Once learners have seen other groups' show-and-tell presentations, ask them to reflect on which group conveyed their message most clearly. What was their message? What did they do to get their message across successfully?

Answers and formative assessment: Open. Encourage learners to specify what it was (e.g. use of voice or gesture) that helped the other learners to get their message across.

Reflection: Refer learners to the learning goals in their books (I can tell other people about using water carefully). See page xxiv for a suggested procedure.

Home learning ideas

Activity: Learners could practise presenting their careful water use message to other family members.

Home–school link: Explain to parents that the learners want to help others understand how to use water more carefully. As parents/care givers, can they help learners present clearly by acting as audience members when the learners are rehearsing their 'show and tell' at home? You may wish to invite parents to attend the learners' presentations if this is part of your school's practice.

4.6 What have we learned about sharing ideas?

LEARNING OBJECTIVES: REFLECTION

1Rf.02 Teamwork: Identify an action that someone else contributed to achieve a shared outcome.

1Rf.03 Personal perspectives: Talk about what has been learned during an activity with support.

LEARNING GOALS

- I can talk about what I learned
- I can talk about how somebody helped me

LEARNING ATTRIBUTES

This lesson gives learners the opportunity to be:

- reflective as learners, developing their ability to learn
- engaged intellectually and socially, ready to make a difference

Resources needed

Learner's Skills Book pages 104–107

Downloadable 4.6 (enlarged version of 'Things I know now about water')

If you took photographs or made recordings when the learners shared their ideas in front of an audience, these would be useful to stimulate reflection

Starter

Good for: Activating learners' understanding of teamwork undertaken as part of the saving water project.

Activity: Explain that during this lesson, we are going to be thinking about all of the things that we have achieved together in our project. Say that you need the learners' help to remember all of the things we did together.

When we shared our ideas, was that something we did by ourselves or did we help each other? *Point to the window if you think that was something we did by ourselves. Point to the door if you thing that was something we helped each other to do in our groups.* Repeat with a range of other activities that the learners did individually or as part of a group. Explain that during this lesson, we are also going to be thinking about all of the things that we have learned during our project about how to save water. Take some early suggestions at this stage.

What do I know now?

Good for: Structuring learners' reflection on what they have found out during the project.

Activity: Support learners in reflecting upon what they have achieved together during this project. Ask them to record these (through drawing and/or writing) in the categories provided. You may wish to distribute enlarged copies of downloadable 4.6 for this.

Answers and formative assessment: Look for responses that demonstrate understanding of the learning during the project.

Differentiation:

Give support by working through some successful responses to this task from previous projects. Help them to find some examples. What did they reflect on well last time? Explain that we are using the same kind of reflection this time – it is just that we are thinking about what we have learned in our new project.

Give extra challenge by asking learners to develop their responses – for example, by asking them to suggest what they would do differently if they were to share their ideas to an audience again.

What have we done together?

Good for: Structuring learners' reflection on their experience of collaborating on the project and how they helped their group.

Activity:

1 Use the activity to allow learners to reflect on the tasks/processes that they performed together during the project, using the images as prompts. Ask learners to discuss what was enjoyable, what was challenging and what they are proud of achieving. They could do this in pairs and then feed back as a class/group.

2 Learners record their answers in writing.

Answers and formative assessment: What did you do *together*? Look for learners' responses that demonstrate reflection on what they achieved with help from other learners at each stage of the project.

Differentiation:

Give support by reassuring learners that it is ok to have found this project challenging. Draw parallels with other tasks that learners have successfully completed that required working together. Share some examples that you have noticed where learners successfully worked together in this project to achieve a goal.

Give extra challenge by asking learners to develop their responses further: *It was hard at first to [action or outcome named] because [obstacle identified]. I enjoyed [group action specified] with my group because [personal response identified]. I am proud that we [action or outcome named] because [successful way of overcoming obstacle and or challenge set out].*

Who helped me?

Good for: Structuring learners' identification of actions that other learners contributed to in order to achieve a shared outcome.

Activity: With the learners, read Sofia's statement about how Marcus helped her. Following this model, learners reflect on who helped them over the course of the project and write their response.

Answers and formative assessment: When were you brave in your project? When did you have an idea for your project? Can the children reflect on their own positive learning behaviours?

When did they help you? How? Can the children specify an action that someone else did that helped the team share their ideas well?

Differentiation:

Give support by prompting learners by mentioning examples that you noticed yourself of where another learner worked closely and cooperatively with them.

Give extra challenge by asking them to develop their responses further. *Before [named person] helped me to [action identified], we could not [group goal identified].* Or *When [named person] helped me to [action identified], we could [group goal identified] because [how the obstacle was removed].*

How have we been good learners?

Good for: Structuring children's reflection on the Cambridge Learner attributes.

Activity: With the children, read Zara and Arun's statement about their positive learning behaviour during the project. Following this model, learners reflect on their own positive learning behaviour over the course of the project and write their response.

Answers and formative assessment: When were you brave in your project? When did you have an idea for your project? Can the learners reflect on their own positive learning behaviours?

When did they help you? How? Can the learners specify an action that someone else did that helped the team share their ideas well?

Plenary

Activity: Share some effective responses to the activities with the whole class. Invite the learners to think about how the collaborative skills they have developed during this project (working together to reach a goal) will help them in future tasks.

Answers and formative assessment: Look for answers that demonstrate appropriate reflection on how their collaborative skills can be applied in a different learning context.

Reflection: Refer learners to the learning goals in their books (I can talk about what I learned. I can talk about how somebody helped me). See page xxiv for a suggested procedure.

Home learning ideas

Activity: Ask the learners to tell parents/care givers (and, if appropriate, extended family members) about their saving water project – what they have learned and what they have achieved as a result of working as part of a team.

Home–school link: Explain to parents/care givers that the saving water project has now come to an end. Encourage them to ask the learners questions about the things that they have learned about why it is important to use water in a responsible way. Encourage them to talk to the learners about what they have been able to achieve in this project because they worked as part of a team.

Taking it further

This project has focused on the importance of clean water for everyone. The learners have used their understanding from research to make a presentation. A logical next step would be to capture this message in writing. Learners could write instruction texts that they performed. The learners' experience of presenting their message to an audience can provide a ready context for writing a range of appropriate instructions. Water is a universal human need. For this reason, a wealth of fiction and poetry has water as a central theme. Explore real-life stories, traditional tales from different cultures, fantasy stories and poetry that explore the need for water as an issue or that capture its place in the natural world.

Understanding the importance of clean water can also be enhanced by out-of-school visits to look at water in the local area – where does it occurs naturally? or where is it and how is it being provided for people? All off-site visits must of course be conducted within your school's safeguarding policy and be thoroughly risk assessed. Visits or secondary sources can be used to develop learners' understanding of water in physical features such as seas, oceans, valleys, lakes and the journeys of rivers. Learners can investigate the water cycle and water as a natural resource. They can also investigate how water supports natural vegetation locally and local rainfall patterns. Learners can investigate key human features where water is important, including canals, ports and harbours.

Learners enjoy practical tasks. An interesting problem-solving exercise would be to provide some water that has other material in it and a variety of filtering equipment. Can they make the water clean again?

It is unfortunately the case that many learners do not have access to clean water. World Water Day is on 22 March, and this would be an excellent opportunity to focus on the right to clean water if it fits in with your school year. UNICEF's figures state that this issue directly impacts the lives of one in five children worldwide. For further information, see the United Nation's page on Water Day, available on the UN website.

Learners who have successfully completed this project will have developed a range of skills and attributes that would enable them to attempt the Cambridge International Primary Global Perspectives Challenge 'Looking after our world' with enhanced confidence.

> Acknowledgements

The authors and publishers acknowledge the following sources of copyright material and are grateful for the permissions granted. While every effort has been made, it has not always been possible to identify the sources of all the material used, or to trace all copyright holders. If any omissions are brought to our notice, we will be happy to include the appropriate acknowledgements on reprinting.

Thanks to the following for permission to reproduce images and videos:

Cover image: Pablo Gallego/Beehive Illustration

Unit 1 Peopleimages/GI; Fizkes/GI; Ariel Skelley/GI; Flashpop/GI; Numismarty/GI; **Unit 2** Seamartini/GI; Jordan Lye/GI; Westend61/GI; Mtreasure/GI; Guido Mieth/GI; Bill Boch/GI; Kipgodi/GI; **Unit 3** Wulingyun/GI; Moof/GI; Tinieder/GI; Alison Wright/GI; Zocha_K/GI; Untitledimages/GI; Education Images/GI; Alexsava/GI; Weiquan Lin/GI; Antagain/GI; **Unit 4** Mariusltu/GI; Alexraths/GI; Gasper_Zalar/GI; Peter Cade/GI; Yevgen Romanenko/GI; Slav/GI; Adisa/GI; Artpipi/GI.

Videos

Unit 1 Ariel Skelley/GI; Realisticfilm/GI(x2); Imagesbazaar/GI(x2); FG Trade/GI(x2); **Unit 2** Kali9/GI(x2); Aleksandarnakic/GI; F.J. Jimenez/GI; Placebo365/GI; Ashley Cooper/GI; Mygreenname/GI; NicolasMcComber/GI; **Unit 3** Ridvan_Celik/GI; Tan Dao Duy/GI; Selamiozalp/GI(x2); Discovery Access/GI; Tan Dao Duy/GI; Zoranm/GI; Simonskafar/GI; Discovery Access/GI; Gsmotion/GI; Discovery Access/GI; BBC Universal/GI; **Unit 4** Hadynyah/GI; Somethingway/GI; Mlharing/GI; Antadi1332/GI; Fivepointsix/GI; Kasipat/GI; Vichie81/GI; Robin Beckham/GI; Jenthakarn Phonrom/GI; Kool99/GI; Kali9/GI; Imgorthand/GI; Alice-Photo/GI; Casarsaguru/GI; Simonkr/GI.

Key GI= Getty Images